Love
Your Child
More

Than You Hate Your Ex

*What Every Divorced Parent
Needs to Know*

DR. LARRY WALDMAN

outskirts
press

Dedication

To Nan:

My greatest love and toughest critic.

We've made it nearly a half-century; let's do another quarter-century.

LFW

Table of Contents

1. Why I Wrote This Book 1
   My Relevant Experience 1
   Sad Statistics 4
   Important Points to Remember in Chapter One 6
2. How We Form our Relationships 7
   We Move Too Fast! 7
   Infatuation is Not Love.. 8
   FORMING OUR RELATIONSHIPS BACKWARDS 9
   Dealing with Issues in a Developing Relationship .. 13
   Important Points to Remember in Chapter Two 14
3. Why Marriages Fail 15
   How We Deal with Conflict 16
   FIVE WAYS TO ARGUE CONSTRUCTIVELY
   WITH YOUR PARTNER... 18
   ACHIEVING "OK" is "GREAT" in MARRIAGE 20
   The Big Four: 21
   Money 21
   Sex 22
   In-Laws.. 23
   Kids 24
   Deal Breakers? 25

Should I Stay in the Marriage "For the Sake of the Kids?" 26
Important Points to Remember in Chapter Three 27

4. Why Second Marriages Fail at Even a Higher Rate 28
   Too Fast—Again 28
   The "Big Four"—Again 29
   Money 29
   Sex 30
   In-Laws 30
   Kids 30
   The Need to Re-Couple—Quickly 31
   Repeating History 31
   Important Points to Remember in Chapter Four 32

5. How to Foster a Healthy Union 34
   Nine Rules for a Strong Marriage 34
   Important Points to Remember in Chapter Five 38

6. What Divorce Looks Like to the Child 39
   Naivete 40
   How the Child Perceives Divorce 41
   Important Points to Remember in Chapter Six 43

7. A Healthy Divorce 44
   What is a Divorce? 44
   Our Adversarial Legal System 47
   Increased Conflict, Time and Money, etc. 49
   Why Such Hate? 50
   The Easier Way—Collaborative Divorce 51
   How CP Works 51
   Important Points to Remember in Chapter Seven 53

8. Parenting through Divorce 54
   FIVE SURE WAYS TO RAISE A RESPONSIBLE
   CHILD 54
   CHANGING UNDESIRABLE BEHAVIOR IN
   OUR KIDS 60
   Overindulged Children 62

Divorced Parenting 64
Parenting Do's (+) and Don'ts (-) 64
Prior to the Separation 64
When to tell the kids...64
What to say to the kids 65
Where the departing parent is going 65
During the Divorce Process 65
Court/legal proceedings.......................................65
Post-Divorce Parenting...66
Where to reside 66
The parenting plan 67
How divorced parents behave when together 67
What divorced parents say to the child about
the other parent 68
Grandparents...70
Managing conflict...71
Contact and visitation 72
After a visit 73
Rules 74
Child as confidante...74
Child as spy 75
Child as messenger...75
Dating after divorce 76
Services for the child 78
Important Points to Remember in Chapter Eight.....79

9. Finding the Right Counselor.................................80
The Stigma of Mental Health..................................80
There is No Education in a Pill...............................82
Where to Find your Counselor 85
What to Look For..86
Ask These Questions 86
Shopping for Mental Health Care...........................87
Important Points to Remember in Chapter Nine.....89

Bibliography...90
Other Books by Dr. Waldman 91

Dr. Waldman Speaks 92
    To the Community and Corporations: 92
    To Mental Health Professionals: 92
    To Attorneys: 92
About Dr. Waldman 93
    Contact Dr. Waldman 94

1

Why I Wrote This Book

"The primary cause for divorce is marriage" — Unknown

My Relevant Experience

FROM 1973 TO 1979 I worked for Scottsdale Schools (Arizona) as a school psychologist. I functioned next as a clinical, forensic psychologist in private practice in Phoenix for the next 37 years. My clients were parents, children, couples and adults. I continue to consult, teach, speak and write.

In the late 90's I chose to work in the arena of forensic psychology. After much reading, clinical consultations and several intensive forensic workshops I specifically became involved in personal injury work and family law. I conducted about 75 custody evaluations over the last 18 years and also served the Maricopa County Superior Court as a Parenting Coordinator (PC) and Therapeutic Interventionist (TI).

When a couple goes through a divorce there may be custodial issues regarding the children—typically one parent having primary custody and decision-making authority or joint-shared custody with equal parenting time and authority. If the issues cannot be resolved by the parents' respective attorneys and the judge wants additional information to make a more informed decision (and the parties can afford it), the judge will appoint an independent, neutral professional to conduct a custody study. From 1998 to 2015 in Maricopa County I was often that expert provider.

In a custody study, as it was called, I interviewed the parents several times and administered psychological tests. I also interviewed the children, if they were old enough, met with relevant parties, like the grandmother, spoke with the teacher, and perhaps the coach. Considerable background material was reviewed, such as any previous psychological treatment of the parents or kids, school reports, and the kids' grades, etc. The process was intense, expensive and lengthy, but I kept it to under 90 days.

A report was compiled with my findings and recommendations, which was sent to the Court and the respective attorneys. The judge would use the report to make his/her findings. Sometimes the case would end with the report and the parties would adopt the recommendations. Other times a hearing in Court would ensue. In that case typically I would be asked to testify. At the conclusion of the trial the judge would offer a final opinion.

In rendering the final decision the judge would occasionally recognize the couples' conflict was not going to end at the trial and would appoint a Parenting Coordinator—PC. I was that practitioner 50-75 times. Back then if a couple had a PC attached to their case, neither parent could file a motion with the Court unless they first met with the PC to attempt to resolve that concern. (The Court was backlogged not because of initial divorce filings but primarily because so many divorce cases were coming back for custody modification.)

As the PC I strived to help the parties communicate appropriately and come to a decision that was "in the child's best interests." Many times I asked this question: "Are you taking this position because you are angry at your ex or because you truly believe this is best for your child." Clearly, this was difficult work but someone with experience had to do it. While not every case ended successfully, a significant number of couples learned to effectively negotiate their issues, "for the sake of the child/ren."

There were also many cases where for one reason or another (drugs, prison or mental health issues, for instance) a parent, married or not, had essentially abandoned the other parent and child but now was interested in re-connecting with their lost child. While most of these parents were fathers a substantial number were long-lost mothers. The parent would petition the Court, often with the aid of a family law attorney, and if the judge believed the parent was fit and serious in their intention, he/she would often appoint a Therapeutic Interventionist—TI. I was that professional about 40 times.

As the TI I would first interview the estranged parent to ensure they were emotionally fit, their motives were pure, and to review the process about to ensue—essentially the time it would take and the expense. (A significant concern was to have an estranged parent re-connect with a child only to abandon the child again, which would do much psychological harm.) In many cases the child was an infant when that parent left and had no recollection of the estranged parent. For that matter, the custodial parent may have married someone and the child believes they already have a father or mother so who was this other parent that wants to meet them and enter their life?

A number of times the case ended quickly. Some parents thought they could walk back into a child's life after being gone for years and immediately begin alternative weekend overnight visitations. Of course, this was not going to happen. The process required that the child would slowly and gradually be re-introduced to their lost parent. If the estranged parent refused to participate in the program, it essentially demonstrated that the parent's commitment to the child was not that strong.

If the estranged parent seemed to be an eligible candidate I next interviewed the custodial parent and the step-parent, if one existed. Obviously, most custodial parents had major reservations about the idea. Finally, I interviewed the child.

Following these interviews visits between the child and lost parent—and between the parents—were held. Again, this was difficult work and certainly not every case was a success but a substantial number of parents and children were able to re-attach. I told parents all the time "the more people who love your child the better."

Doing this demanding work of a custody evaluator, PC and TI gave me a first-hand, in-depth view of what goes on in divorce and how the children are Impacted by the process.

Sad Statistics

Maricopa County, which includes Phoenix and Scottsdale, has the dubious "honor" of being the divorce capital of the world. More divorces are filed here than in any other county—surpassing Clark county, which includes Las Vegas, years ago. Reportedly the transiency of the area (relatively few people were born in Phoenix—most are transplants); the stress of the move—away from family and friends; a lower wage scale; the lack of industry; and thousands of couples coming to the "Valley of the Sun" to escape the cold and snow of the North bringing their issues with them, all contribute to the high divorce rate.

Given the above facts, in my professional career spanning nearly a half-century, I have seen hundreds of families go through the tumultuous process of divorce. Moreover, I have witnessed perhaps a thousand or more children struggle with the emotional trauma of having their parents separate and divorce.

The national data is a bit unclear (the CDC) but somewhere between one-third and one-half of all marriages in the US fail. The majority of these divorces occur within the first five years. (Statistically, if a couple makes it five years there is a good chance the marriage will last—but, of course, there is no guarantee.) Recent demographic data indicates there has been a noticeable increase in the divorce rate among "empty nesters"—middle aged unions breaking once the young adult children leave the home. Interestingly, when one or both of the parties have been married previously one-half to two-thirds of those relationships ultimately collapse.

The US, by far, has the highest divorce rate on the planet. To me this is a national travesty. The angst and cost of a divorce is huge. Moreover, the emotional toll on the involved children is immeasurable.

A well-known but sad fact in the human services arena is that given our current high level of transiency in our relationships more children today in the US are living with a single parent, stepparent or grandparent(s) than children residing with both natural parents (Anderson, 2014). This is not to say that any of the above non-traditional family constellations are inherently bad. What this statistic does mean, though, is millions of children have experienced the trauma of divorce, the break-up of their parents, and/or the loss of the connection with a natural parent. Perhaps this may also play a role in the high suicide rate in teens today.

Children are the future. What does it mean for our society if more than half of our children have been traumatized?! This may explain, at least in part, why the high divorce rate continues.

During my work I saw firsthand the hurt and anger of betrayal by a once–loved partner; the terror and anxiety of domestic violence and abuse; the frustration in being incapable of communicating or resolving ongoing issues; and the fear of being unable to afford suitable housing or food following separation and divorce. Moreover, I have witnessed children whom are confused, anxious, emotionally destabilized and literally traumatized by their parents' divorce and the post- divorce proceedings.

If that wasn't enough for these unfortunate children caught in the turmoil of divorce, I have seen many grandparents, typically the parents of the father, who essentially lost their relationship with their grandchild(ren) due to the split of their son and daughter-in-law. As a grandfather of three kids, and the parent of two fathers, I lament that too often in divorce the connection the child has with his/her grandparents is ignored. This adds to the child's sense of loss and to the overall stress to the family constellation.

My goal, then, in this book is to discuss and try to decrease the high incidence of divorce and reduce the associated psychological distress on parents, grandparents and children in the process of divorce. In order to do this the following topics will be addressed:

- How do we form our relationships?
- Why marriages fail
- Why second marriages fail at even a higher rate
- How to foster a healthy union
- What divorce looks like to the child
- How to have a healthy divorce
- Quality parenting through divorce
- Finding the right counselor

Important Points to Remember in Chapter One

1. 33%-48% of marriages in the US will end in divorce.
2. About 65% of marriages that involve a previously-married spouse will fail.
3. The US has the highest divorce rate in the world—by a landslide!
4. In divorce everyone suffers—the couple, the grandparents and most especially the kids.

2

How We Form our Relationships

"Examine the rope before you tie the knot"—Waldman

I AM CONVINCED that who we marry and how we form our primary relationship is the central reason why marriages work or falter.

We Move Too Fast!

You wouldn't buy a house without thoroughly inspecting it. By the same token, you wouldn't purchase a car without test driving it. Whom we choose to marry is probably one of most important decisions—if not <u>the</u> most important decision— we will make in our life. Yet far too often today many people "fall in love" and form a relationship in a matter of a few weeks with extremely limited vital information. I swear some folks do more research in selecting their next I-phone than in choosing their life-long partner.

I cannot tell you how often patients told me this story:

"We met at a bar (or party). We slept together that first night. We moved in together within two months."

Internet sites, like Tinder, encourage quick "hook-ups." Popular TV shows, such as The Bachelor, The Bachelorette and The 90-Day Engagement, all convey the ridiculous message that we can find our "soul-mate," life-long partner, in a matter of weeks—in a game-like atmosphere, no less. Not surprisingly, very few of these TV connections result in a satisfactory long-term relationship. While it may make for interesting reality TV (for some), it fails to teach that selecting a worthy mate takes time and effort.

Couples who rush into romance quickly become committed sexually, emotionally and often financially (like buying a bed or sofa together) and the relationship takes on its own inertia. They have not had the time (or inclination) to fully "vet" their prospective life partner. Moreover, while "issues" may well come to light during this whirlwind courtship the partner is likely to ignore or minimize the concern(s) because the attachment and commitment are already in place. For example:

"He seems to drink a lot …. but he's soooo good in bed."

"Her father is in prison and her mother is crazy ….but she's sooooo good in bed."

Bottom line: Many people confuse "falling in lust" with "falling in love."

Infatuation is Not Love

Physical attraction ignites most relationships. It's that first glimpse that gets our attention and causes us to want to get to know that person better. That tingling feeling we get when we begin to connect with someone we're attracted to and the thrill we enjoy from early sexual encounters is called infatuation—or "chemistry." It's real. It truly is a change in our brain chemistry—endorphins abound. It's evolutionary. This is what makes us want to breed and re-populate the species.

Infatuation, unfortunately, doesn't last. Limited research (Agape 2019) suggests it can last from six to 18 months—if you're lucky. Infatuation slowly erodes, just like our youth. Obviously, it is not what a long-term relationship should be based upon. This is another reason why most divorces occur within the first five years.

By the second anniversary the sex is no longer new and the couple had better learn to communicate, respect and trust each other, be considerate of each other's needs, and enjoy each other's company

---

or the union is in big trouble. Interestingly, in a healthy relationship the sexual attraction may dim slightly (but hopefully never go away!) but the positive feelings each person has for their partner continues to grow.

The metaphor that marital sex is like the cherry atop the sundae is apt: If the ice cream supporting the cherry is fresh and flavorful, you have a very tasty dessert. On the other hand, if the ice cream below the cherry is old and re-frozen the confection is inedible. In other words, long-term good sex comes from a solid relationship—but a solid relationship isn't made from good sex. For many they have it backwards.

(I refer to heterosexual couples in this book but in my professional experience same-sex couples experience the same issues—only with additional discrimination.)

Here is an article I wrote on this topic which was published in the local Phoenix media:

FORMING OUR RELATIONSHIPS BACKWARDS

By

Larry F. Waldman, Ph.D., ABPP

The divorce rate in the U.S. continues to hover around 50 percent and the dissolution incidence when one or both of the parties have been previously married is about 65 percent. This is a national travesty. The amount of emotional angst and money spent, not to mention the extent of trauma brought to the involved children, is immeasurable.

Finding a partner today has never been easier. There are numerous websites which facilitate making a connection with a prospective mate. Two generations ago one typically met their prospective spouse at a bar, dance, or was "fixed up" by a mutual friend or family member. Today a few mouse clicks may be all that is needed to begin a relationship.

Despite the technology-aided match-making, relationships are not lasting any longer than before—and things are likely to get worse. The reason for this is that more than ever before we are developing our relationships in a backward manner.

Ask any relationship expert or any couple happily married for a while and they will say that a successful long-term marriage is based, in large part, on compatible values and principles, positive personality characteristics, commitment to the relationship, effective communication, and enjoying each other's company. While sex is important, it is not part of the basic foundation of the relationship; passion is a wonderful benefit of a solid relationship.

Not that long ago, couples courted. Premarital sex was frowned upon. In some cultures the couple was chaperoned during the dating phase. While all this sounds terribly outdated by today's standards, these couples were, in fact, building a firm foundation for their future relationship, as they focused on the primary tenets of a successful long-term union. Diagrammatically, successful relationships look like a **pyramid**, with the union soundly grounded on shared values and principles:

Sex

Communication

Commitment

Personality Characteristics

Solid, Basic Values and Principles

Today, many relationships are formed in a backward manner. Given the ease of connecting, "hook-ups" are common. Some current sites, like Tinder, are expressly aimed at creating sexual liaisons.

In a relationship that begins primarily due to a sexual connection, all those important factors, like values and commitment, become secondary. The sexual attraction blinds the individual to problems that may exist in their bedmate with regard to personal values, personality characteristics, communication, etc. Such a relationship, diagrammatically, looks like an inverted **pyramid**, balancing precariously on sex:

Solid, Basic Values and Principles

Personality Characteristics

Communication
Commitment

Sex

Is it any wonder, then, that relationships founded on lust ultimately teeter and collapse? Let's get back to the "good old days" and form solid, long-lasting intimate relationships right side up.

If you are in a relationship and are contemplating marriage, consider the following:

What is his/her family like?

Do his/her parents respect each other?

Does he/she respect his/her parents?

What is his/her view on the sanctity of marriage?

How does he/she communicate?

How does he/she handle money?

How does he/she run his/her house or apartment?

How does/would he/she raise children?

How does he/she handle change, frustration, and disappointment?

How does he/she resolve conflict?

How willing is he/she to consider your needs?

Does he/she overuse drugs and/or alcohol?

How willing is he/she to compromise?

All of these questions, and perhaps several more, need to be investigated before one decides to make a life-long commitment to another person. Simply being good in bed doesn't cut it. A relationship founded primarily on lust will last, if you are lucky (and really sensual), at most 18 months. Successful long-term relationships, per the **"Pyramid,"** must be built from the ground up.

The salient points of this article are that long-term, solid, healthy relationships are based on similar values, compatible personalities, communication, commitment and **TRUST**. Investigating and developing these attributes takes **TIME**. Sex should be the "cherry on the top" once all these factors are in place, not the foundation of the pairing. First, become good friends, then lovers.

Please pay close attention to the questions asked at the end of the above article. These issues are central to the health and longevity of a marriage. You must investigate them in your prospective partner and address any problems if they become apparent. If you do your "homework" before you make a life-long commitment, your marriage will go much smoother.

I remember a case with a couple with very different views on religion. While they were very much "in love," early on, the husband, essentially an atheist, could not abide many of the customs and traditions of his wife and her family. He thus chose not to participate in them. Very quickly this became a major sore point in their relationship, compounded by the wife's family dislike for their son-in-law. Due to this issue, and a few others, within two-three years the marriage dissolved. Unfortunately, by then they had a daughter. A messy custody issue ensued primarily over the religious training of the little girl. The Court appointed me to conduct the custody study, which convinced me this child was going to face a childhood fraught with conflict. If this couple had only discussed their theological differences in depth early on in their relationship, this misfortune could have been avoided.

In olden days, and in some cultures currently, there was/is a designated, extensive courting period. During this time the couple goes on many dates, often with a chaperone, and the families of each partner meet regularly. While this practice seems completely outdated today, this procedure afforded the opportunity for the couple to truly get to know each other without the confusion and interference of sex. Also, important issues, like culture, religion, and inter – family relations etc. were already in place. Interestingly, the divorce rate for arranged marriages, is significantly lower than the norm because, I believe, the foundation of the relationship (the base of the **"pyramid"**) has been firmly established.

Dealing with Issues in a Developing Relationship

After working with probably a thousand couples I am completely convinced that the issues that continue to plague the union, and often are the factors that lead to divorce, were evident early in the (too brief) courting phase. Unfortunately, most couples were too much "in lust" to recognize or address those concerns early on.

No one is perfect. We all have our quirks. Marriage involves com-promise and acceptance. The perfect "prince charming" or the flawless "princess" exist only in fairy tales.

What if you see a problem with a potential partner? You must talk about it and address it. If you are unsuccessful at this point, you must see a marital counselor.

Some issues may not be resolvable. For example, if there is a history of genetic anomalies in the family, such as learning disabilities, attention deficit disorder (ADD), autism, depression, addiction, sociopathy, medical issues, etc. the odds are higher that children from this gene pool may inherit some of those problems. The partner must recognize these concerns and make an informed choice.

Each person should also give some thought as to their own

background, their own issues, and why they are attracted to their prospective partner. Freud noted the first relationship we have with the opposite sex is with our opposite sex parent. Therefore, I recommend that all couples considering marriage, with obvious issues or not, consider pre-marital counseling.

Unfortunately today with the unwarranted stigma of mental health, (more on that in the last chapter) psychologists and other mental health providers unfortunately do little prevention work. Most of what we do is what I call "mopping up,"—trying to clean up the mess that has already been created. In my career I count six couples with whom I did pre-marital work. With two of them I suggested they think twice before "tying the knot."

Important Points to Remember in Chapter Two

1. We couple too fast and don't vet our prospective partner.
2. We fall "in lust" not "in love" and miss or ignore the problems in the relationship.
3. Healthy long-term unions are founded on similar values, compatible personalities, joint interests, commitment and trust—not just good sex.
4. All couples considering marriage should seek pre-marital counseling.

3

Why Marriages Fail

"A happy marriage is not so much about how compatible you are but how you deal with the incompatibility" — G. Levinger

GIVEN THAT ONE-THIRD to one-half of marriages dissolve when both parties once were in love (or at least in lust), and may even have had children, can be difficult to fathom. Nevertheless, as previously discussed, most of these failed relationships came with significant issues from the very beginning. Aside from these built-in problems, major problems can develop during the union.

A sustainable marriage requires the successful blending of two persons, of opposite genders (not always, of course), from different backgrounds, some with different cultures and traditions, occasionally of different races, often with different levels of education, and usually raised in contrasting environments. Given all this, it seems like a miracle that only about half of unions fail.

Recently my wife, Nan, and I had an interchange that highlighted for me the innate difference between men and women:

I have a 1989 BMW convertible which I bought new. I love the car but it is beginning to show its age. Over dinner several weeks ago I said to Nan that I would like to spiff up the car—new top, fix the upholstery, improve the suspension, maybe a new paint job.

Her response was, "Are you nuts?! Why would you spend all that money on a car that's nearly 30 years old!? What a waste!" The discussion basically ended there.

About three weeks later Nan tells me she was shopping with a girlfriend and they stopped at a high-end jewelry store. She decided then it was time to update her diamond wedding ring. (Ironically, she was talking about the same amount of money as I was regarding the BMW.)

I said, "Dear, your idea of upgrading your wedding ring sounds as crazy to me as you feel about me improving my car."

(Like what usually happens in our union, we negotiated a pretty good deal with the jeweler. "Happy wife—happy life." Recently, though, my BMW also got its overhaul. How could Nan deny me?!)

When I tell this story to men they think Nan was unfair. Alternatively, when I mention it to women they agree with her wholeheartedly.

The lesson here is that men and women see the world differently. Partners in marriage must recognize these differences, be willing to communicate openly, negotiate honestly, and be amenable to compromise. Unfortunately, only about half the population can do that.

How We Deal with Conflict

A relationship doesn't exist that doesn't have issues. There is just no such thing. A healthy relationship is one where those issues are managed. Unfortunately, most of us aren't trained in communication or problem resolution.

It doesn't take long in most relationships for the central problems to become apparent. For most couples the issues they argued about during the courting phase are essentially the same ones they wrestle with when living in the senior center—if they make it that far.

Most couples don't address their issues until they're in them. For example, I used to tell my clients, "The best time to talk about concerns in the bedroom is when you are in the kitchen" (and are not in the emotion of the moment).

When one of those ugly issues arise typically voices are raised and nasty statements are made which cut deeply. Sometimes there is "stone-walling" (refusal to discuss the topic—more often seen in husbands, I contend) and the ever-dangerous threats of leaving or divorce. Usually a strained period of uncomfortable silence and distance follows such interchanges. As these episodes continue the marital bond begins to erode. This inability for the couple to resolve or settle their issues is, I believe, the primary reason for the high divorce rate in this country.

Over time the couple begins to recognize they can't manage any of their major problems. Certain issues begin to fester. There may be reluctance to even bring up any issue for fear of another hurtful, unsatisfactory exchange. When a partner begins to believe that there will be no resolution to their concerns this is the beginning of the end. The on-going conflict with no satisfactory conclusion leads to disappointment, frustration, anger, additional bickering, and, finally, resignation.

There often is less arguing now because the partner has decided there is no likelihood of any change. When one, or both, of the partners stop caring the union is definitely in jeopardy.

At some time during this period of resignation a partner will experience what therapists call the "emotional disconnect." This is where the partner may look like all is OK, but they are just going through the motions. I had several cases where a partner was completely flummoxed by their mate telling them they wanted a divorce; they had no idea, whatsoever, that anything was so wrong. In truth, their partners had emotionally disconnected from them months, and in some cases, years before.

Occasionally a disconnected partner will precipitate a crisis—like an affair—to finally bring an end to the relationship. A colleague once told me that he prefers to work with couples whom are still arguing because at least they both care about the relationship and still believe it can work.

Here is another quite relevant article of mine on how to "fight fair," which was also published.

FIVE WAYS TO ARGUE CONSTRUCTIVELY WITH YOUR PARTNER

By

Larry F. Waldman, Ph.D., ABPP

The divorce rate hovers at around 50 percent which, I contend, is a national tragedy. A major reason for this statistic is that most couples have not learned how to settle their issues.

1) "Discussions" are necessary in any relationship to allow it to grow but the process must be constructive. Destructive arguing consists of raised voices, demeaning, and discounting. Destructive arguing leads to resentment and ongoing issues which never end. With constructive arguing the goal is resolution or compromise— not finding a winner or a loser.

2) Most marital spats are spontaneous—where one party is up-set and the other party is caught off guard. Resolution is rarely achieved in these "ambush" arguments. Couples should make an appointment to discuss an issue.

3) During a scheduled discussion one—and only one—issue should be dealt with at a time. When most couples argue usu-ally within seconds every other issue the couple possesses gets dumped into the conversation. Resolution then is impossible. No "side tracking" (getting off the issue); no "bombs" (making an inflammatory comment); and no "digging up the museum" (bringing up an old sore issue) should be allowed. Each partner must strive to speak only about the circumscribed issue until it is resolved.

4) It is easier to settle issues when couples learn to speak con-cretely. The questions that need to be considered are: "What does it look like? What would I see?" For example, if the wife tells the husband she would like him to be "more affectionate," the hus-band should not respond, "You don't know what you are talking about; I' m as affectionate as the next guy." The husband should instead say, "Dear, if I were more affectionate, what would it look like? What would we see?" The wife, then, could answer with

whatever behavior she would view as affectionate—hold her hand, write her a love note, bring flowers, bathe the baby, rub her back, fix the sink, arrange a date (including securing the baby-sitter), etc.

5) For most couples arguing entails over-shouting, interrupting, and negative body language. If one party is silent, they are typically not listening to their partner but are focused on their response as soon as they can get a word in edgewise. The paraphrase technique involves having one partner state their position for no more than 60 seconds while the other partner quietly listens. At the end of the minute, before the second partner can offer their rebuttal, they must first paraphrase their partner's position. This forces the partner to really "hear." Once they stated their partner's view, then they get their 60 seconds and the other partner then must listen and paraphrase.

Couples who adopt these five rules quickly learn that their discussions can be constructive, issues can be resolved, and their relationship can flourish.

If couples learn to use these guidelines to manage their conflict, their relationship will grow, as they recognize that issues can be resolved. This might even put a dent in the ridiculous divorce rate in this country.

By the way, if you just had a fight with your partner, don't call your Mom in Dubuque (Iowa) and complain to her about you mate. This will only serve to worry your parents and add tension to the connection between your parents and your spouse. Besides, an hour later you might be having make-up sex but back in Iowa they are still chafing. If you have to talk to somebody, see a friend (you don't socialize as a couple with) or, better yet, contact a mental health provider.

Below is another article I wrote regarding marital communication:

ACHIEVING "OK" is "GREAT" in MARRIAGE

By

Larry F. Waldman Ph.D., ABPP

Ironworks Inc. and Acme Steel have been doing business together for twenty-five years. Ironworks manufactures steel widgets and Acme sells raw steel. These two companies have worked together for all this time for two basic reasons: 1. They need each other. 2. The money is right. Ironworks believes they are buying their raw materials at a reasonable cost and Acme believes they are selling their steel at an acceptable price.

Since these companies are privately-held businesses, they each desire to make increased profits. However, if Acme notifies Ironworks that next month the price per ton of steel will increase 50%, Ironworks may grudgingly make their next order but will immediately begin searching for a new supplier. By the same token, if Ironworks notifies Acme that next month they will only pay 50% less per ton of steel, Acme may reluctantly fill the next order but will immediately begin searching for a new customer. Thus, if either company substantially alters the price in their favor, a business relationship that had endured a quarter-century will collapse.

This analogy regarding these two companies closely relates to marriage: When the above-noted companies conducted business with each other such that both were satisfied (not necessarily overjoyed) with the financial arrangement, the business relationship prospered. When either company attempted to seek a greater profit—a "win"—the relationship dissolved. Similarly, when couples interact in a spirit of compromise and cooperation the union flourishes. However, when one or both partners argues to "win," frequently issues edicts or ultimatums, or threatens divorce if they don't get their way, the marriage is threatened. Like the long-term business relationship between Ironworks Inc. and Acme Steel, marriage works best when each party strives for mutual satisfaction—not a personal win. Therefore, achieving "ok" in marriage is "great."

The Big Four:

Research indicates that the four top issues which plague most marriages are—in this order—money, sex, in-laws and kids. (I joke that if, god forbid, I needed to find another partner, I would seek a wealthy, orphaned, childless, nymphomaniac.)

MONEY

People have different beliefs and goals with respect to money. There will likely be a significant difference in risk-taking, for example. Financial management (Who pays the bills? Do we have separate checking accounts?) and goals (Do we buy a house as soon as possible? When do we begin preparing for retirement?), for example, must be discussed thoroughly before the "walk down the aisle." Today, I recommend that you check your prospective partner's credit rating to get a sense of their financial responsibility.

Living together without sufficient income to meet basic needs is quite stressful to a relationship. There is anger and blame. The tendency to vent frustration on your partner is high. It's hard to make a marriage work without sufficient funds when both partners are working long hours, are exhausted, and have no money to recreate or relax.

Even when the income is sufficient problems can occur when partners disagree on what to do with the money —save it, invest, fix the house, by a new car, take a vacation, or purchase the new toy, etc. In my marriage seminars attendees are asked to separately write their answer to the following: "If $10,000 suddenly fell into your hands, what would you do with it?" If one partner says bank it and the other suggests buy a boat, the couple has considerable work to do regarding their financial aspirations.

Couples must come to terms about money early on or they will continue to struggle with this issue throughout their time together. I have seen too many marriages where the husband attempts to monitor and control his wife's spending and the wife, resenting the overmanagement, continues to spend money behind her husband's back. Unions will crumble when a partner feels they have been betrayed monetarily.

Nan's family had more money than mine. She liked to shop. I saw early on this could be a problem. We discussed the issue and Nan agreed, somewhat reluctantly at first, that she would handle the household finances. I believed I did not want to control Nan's spending because that would lead to other problems. If she had to balance the family budget and clearly saw how her spending affected that budget, she would manage her spending on her own. This is exactly what occurred. Forty-eight years later Nan is a fabulous money manager.

I have used this notion often in my psychology practice. In many cases where one spouse is complaining about how their partner is spending money I recommended that the "spending partner" take over the budget and pay the bills. Often I initially met with resistance ("He'll break the bank!!") but for the most part, most of my client-couples that took that advice did well. Not trying to control your partner but instead giving them control often is a satisfying resolution to a sticky issue.

SEX

For most couples, especially younger ones, the primary concern here is frequency, not quality. Typically the husband desires intimacy more often—but not always. Like the above money issue, too many men pressure their partners for sex. I could never understand why would you want to have sex with someone whom has been coerced into it?

Not surprisingly, the same concept regarding control of the money works in this arena as well. I counselled many couples that were struggling with sexual frequency that the "less-sexual" partner should be the one to decide when intimacy occurred. Of course, again I met with resistance—"I might as well become a monk!" Yet, when one partner has the ability to have sex or not, typically that partner chooses to be sensual far more often than when they were cajoled into it—and the sex is often much better!

If the relationship was founded on sexual gratification and now your partner is much less interested in sex than you, the union is obviously in trouble. Conflict in this arena has ruined many marriages. This is probably another reason why so many marriages fail within the first five years.

As a senior, I know first-hand—professionally and personally—that as we age our interest in sex changes. This is true for both women and especially men. Moreover, with all the medical issues we may be experiencing (like high blood pressure and/or diabetes), the medications we are taking, being overweight and de-conditioned, sex becomes much less important—if not impossible.

I had cases where the roles in the relationship flipped: Early on, the husband wanted sexual activity whenever possible and pushed his mate to cooperate but around the time he passed the half-century mark in age he essentially became asexual. Now the wife was the one seeking physical contact.

In a session the husband shared that due to his age, physical condition, and the blood pressure and anti-depressant medications he was on, he no longer could achieve or maintain an erection. Thus, to avoid frustration he gave up sexual activity altogether—to his partner's chagrin.

I suggested to them that sex, especially in marriage, is not just a physical act. It brings physical and emotional bonding to the relationship. "Old sex" can be better and certainly more meaningful than a brief fling. Thus, I recommended to the couple that they "make an appointment" to be together. They should kiss, touch and caress.

They took my advice and brought back physical closeness into their relationship. Interestingly, with no expectations and the pressure off, the husband was occasionally able to perform. Funny how that works.

IN-LAWS

With your partner comes their parents and family. It's a package deal. Hopefully this is good because there are now more people that can support and even love you—and your kids, if you choose to procreate. Sometimes, though, the relationship with the in-laws is more tenuous. (Now the in-laws are "out-laws.")

Issues with in-laws usually come from three general areas: They don't care enough. They care too much. They are hyper-critical.

Some newly married partners wish their partner's folks were more helpful and involved, like being invited to dinner now and then. Help from in-laws can be especially welcome when the kids arrive.

On the other hand, some in-laws become so involved they are overly-demanding and intrusive. They may even infringe on the couple's privacy. Like expecting them over for dinner every Sunday night. I had one case where the wife's mother would often come over unannounced.

If the partner is critical of their in-laws and/or the in-laws are unhappy with their new son/daughter-in-law there will undoubtedly be significant family tension. One of the worst things you can do in a union, though, is to put your partner between you and their parents. ("Tell your Mom to stop being so pushy.") It is a most uncomfortable spot to be in. You are stuck; you can't win. Here is where "agreeing to disagree" is very useful.

Managing a "sticky" in-law issue is tricky. It takes open, tactful communication with your partner and possibly with your in-law. What is foremost, as always, is appreciating and supporting your partner. "Acceptance" may be necessary in this arena.

KIDS

Generally, kids tend to cement a relationship. The mutual experience of going through the gestation, birth and the process of rearing a human being usually bonds a couple. However, I have seen couples where the mother felt father was not "pulling his weight" with respect to the childcare. Over time this can certainly stress a couple. Having children markedly changes a marriage.

Sociological data also indicates if the couple has a child before they are married or before they are about 21 years old, the union has a higher likelihood of dissolving. This is clearly due to the additional stress—emotionally, physically and financially—a baby brings to young marriage where the parties haven't had the time to settle in and/or the parties are essentially children themselves. Also, if the child unfortunately has a substantial health problem and/or a developmental delay, the marriage is super-stressed. Finally, if the couple has not discussed parenting ahead of time, there will likely be incidents where one parent is upset about how the other parent handled—or mishandled—a situation with the child.

Whether spanking should be employed as a method of child discipline is a hot area of contention between many couples and therefore needs to be thoroughly discussed before the "little bundle of joy" arrives. Typically, most parents parent the way they were parented. (For that matter, most people are married the same way their folks were married.) In general, if you were spanked as a child, you'll advocate for that. You came out OK, right!? On the other hand, if physical discipline was not part of your childhood, you likely will disavow corporal punishment.

Again, when you plan to purchase something big—like a car, appliance, some electronic equipment—you research it before you buy it. Sadly, most parents-to-be haven't read one book on child development or child discipline before they bring the kid home from the hospital. (Reading a book or two on marriage wouldn't be a bad idea also.) When that "precious little ball of love" gets older they will strive to work one parent against the other. Don't fall for that.

You will probably also get advice—requested or not—from your parents and the in(out?)-laws on all facets of childcare. I suggest you listen to them, do some of your own research, and then do what you <u>and your partner</u> think is best.

Deal Breakers?

When we commit to marry someone we make some basic assumptions:

- My partner will keep me physically safe.
- My partner will treat me with respect.
- My partner will be sexually faithful.
- My partner will be financially open and honest.
- My partner will keep our personal life secret.
- My partner will not overuse drugs or alcohol.
- My partner will seek help for any major medical or mental problem.

Physical abuse, emotional/verbal abuse, sexual infidelity, significant financial indiscretions (like compulsive gambling), emotional infidelity, drug abuse and untreated mental illness cannot be tolerated in a marriage. They all are breaches of **TRUST**. At the first sign of any of these issues the problem must be addressed and marital counseling must immediately ensue. If the issue is ignored, the core of the relationship—TRUST—is in jeopardy. Left untreated, these issues will cause years of chaos and anguish.

The above issues, in my view, if untreated, are **deal breakers**. If your partner refuses to seek help, leave the residence or demand your spouse leave. After several weeks of separation if your partner still refuses to address the problem(s), it is time to end the union.

I know I've said it before, but these major issues rarely spring up after the wedding. In most cases signs of these significant concerns were apparent during the courting phase but, as we already know, they were ignored or dismissed. Obviously, the best time to address the issues is before "the walk down the aisle." If the issues are not resolved, it is also far easier to exit the relationship before papers are signed or the kids come.

Should I Stay in the Marriage "For the Sake of the Kids?"

This question has been posed to me several times. My answer is, "It depends, but generally, no."

If a couple vows to maintain their relationship and behave essentially as if they were still a loving couple, then yes. This entails no more arguing than before, sleeping in the same bedroom, essentially carrying on as if nothing emotionally has occurred. Not many couples can pull this off. Additionally, living in a loveless relationship is extremely difficult. Parents deserve to be in love.

During my career I saw several couples whom regularly had screaming tirades and treated each other disrespectfully for years. When I asked them why they hadn't considered divorce their answer was, "We stay together for the sake of the kids." My response was: "You're not doing the children a favor."

Children live what they learn. Parents overtly teach their kids many, many things: How to eat; how to dress; how to brush your teeth and wash your hair; how to be polite; how to share; how to manage conflict, etc., etc. Much of what we teach them, though, is indirect. For example, you are the only Mom or Dad they knew. Unless the child earns a master's degree in child development, it is most likely the child will someday parent much like the way they were parented.

Similarly, your marriage is the only one, or at least the first, that the child experienced. Therefore, what the child takes from that union will largely dictate what their future marriage will look like. Thus, if the child sees chaos in their parents' union, the child's ultimate marriage is also likely to be unstable. Clearly, the child has not been done a favor—and the ugly statistics regarding marriage and divorce continue to roll along. Nevertheless, sometimes a clean divorce between poorly matched partners is the best thing for the child.

Important Points to Remember in Chapter Three

1. The inability to manage conflict dooms many marriages. Couples must learn to communicate and negotiate effectively—and come to "acceptance" with some issues.
2. In marriage the goal of a discussion is to seek resolution not a win.
3. Money, Sex, In-laws and Kids are the "Big 4" areas of marital stress for most couples.
4. Couples must discuss in depth the above issues—and any others unique to that couple—before they exchange vows.
5. Couples must do their research on marriage, managing money, and raising kidsetc. before they undoubtedly confront challenges in those areas later on.
6. Deal breaking issues must be addressed and treated. They cannot be ignored. Left untreated, they are legitimate reasons for divorce.
7. Generally, staying in an unsatisfying marriage "for the sake of the kids" is a contradiction in terms.

4

Why Second Marriages Fail at Even a Higher Rate

"The most dangerous food a person can eat—wedding cake!"—Waldman

COMMON SENSE SUGGESTS that if a person is about to remarry they are older, wiser, know what they want and don't want, and have learned from past experiences. Thus, the divorce rate for second (and subsequent) marriages should be substantially lower than for first marriages. Despite the logic this is absolutely **NOT** the case! Demographic data (the CDC) clearly indicates that about 65% (two-thirds) of second marriages falter and the numbers for subsequent marriages are even worse.

Consider all the angst these failed unions create. Moreover, the stress the involved children must endure having to live through two (or more) divorces is beyond comprehension.

Why do these relationships fail so often?

Too Fast—Again

When I was preparing to enter the forensic field in the 90's I attended a seminar in which a family law judge presented. I was struck by something he said:

"For most parties when they come to the Court to sign their final divorce papers they already have a new committed partner at their side."

Going through a divorce is an extremely difficult and emotional experience. Social science denotes that divorce rates highest on the "Stress Scale." A person you once loved has rejected you. Your self-esteem is at an all-time low.

In this condition if someone starts sending you messages that you're OK, nice and even attractive, that is like cocaine!! You need and want as much of that attention as you can get! Within a flash you dump those lousy, ugly feelings of self-repute and jump into a new relationship. As we have seen too often with first marriages, once again you dive into a pairing without taking the time to fully examine your new partner. Yet now you—and possibly your new partner—may have significant additional obligations in your/their life.

The "Big Four"—Again

Another major reason for the collapse of these relationships is that second marriages have all the issues inherent in first marriages—with the added baggage of the first union.

MONEY

As discussed previously, money is a huge factor in relationships. With the cost of a previous divorce, probably having had to move, and with spousal maintenance and child support obligations, the financial status for most parties in a subsequent marriage is typically worse and much more complicated than in the first union.

I had a case where a couple, both with two kids, had divorced and remarried. The husband dutifully paid child support to his ex for their kids but the wife's ex was not as responsible with his support payment for their kids. Money was tight and the wife was galled to see her current husband regularly send much-needed money to a woman she didn't know. The wife was angry that her husband was paying so much and the husband was irate that his wife was allowing her ex to get away without paying his fair share. Sadly, they didn't have the funds to hire an attorney to bring the wife's ex back to court. The union soon eroded.

SEX

Essentially the same issues exist regarding sex in subsequent relationships as are in first marriages. Obviously, the major difference is that someone else was there previously. I had cases where one partner moved in with the other partner but insisted that they purchase a new bed—or at least a new mattress—so not to sleep where the ex once slept. A few clients thought that was a waste of money but the smart ones complied with that request. Comparisons are inevitable—which may or may not be OK. "Did you have that problem with Carol?" (the ex) usually doesn't lead to a healthy discussion.

IN-LAWS

As discussed previously, the new partner also likely comes with a family so once more you will have to deal with another set of in-laws. Additionally, don't forget that while you may have divorced your ex you didn't divorce your ex in-laws. You must appreciate the connection between your kids and their grandparents and facilitate it. The kids didn't ask for the divorce and they certainly shouldn't have to lose their relationship with their grandparents. Of course, it would also be great if a close relationship could be fostered between the kids and your new in-laws. I'll say it again: "The more people who love your kids the better." Nevertheless, the in-law situation following a divorce which includes kids gets much more complicated. (Deciding whose house you go to for Thanksgiving can be really challenging.)

KIDS

As noted above, kids typically cement a relationship. On the other hand, step-kids can act like a chisel to crack the union. Generally, the older the kids the bigger the problems. If the new union forms relatively close to the separation/divorce, the kids may assume (rightly or often wrongly) that the stepparent caused their parents' split. The relationship between kids and the step-parent, then, is seriously strained. Sadly, sometimes these hard feelings are stoked by the ex.

Pre-teens and certainly adolescents naturally tend to be more challenging to authority. If they view the step-parent as an interloper and the source of much of the family distress, they are more likely to act out. Be prepared for, "I don't have to listen to you; you're not my Mother/Father!" Again, some ex's have been known to prompt their kids to disrespect their step-parent.

If this weren't enough, sometimes in these "blended families" the partners criticize each other regarding their parenting skills and frequently point out how their kids are misbehaving. By now it should be obvious that if not handled well, older step-kids can easily fracture a marriage.

The Need to Re-Couple—Quickly

Following a separation you naturally feel alone. It is uncomfortable to be "uncoupled." Few people enjoy traveling, going to a movie or to a nice restaurant by themselves. To avoid this discomfort some individuals secure their new partner as quickly as possible—sometimes even before they have left the first relationship. Obviously, rushing to re-couple does not bode well for the new union.

REPEATING HISTORY

While the above six reasons explain to a large degree why second marriages fail I believe this is not the final answer. Have you ever heard someone say: "I got divorced but I now realize the significant role I played in the demise of our marriage?" In my career I never heard anything like that. Instead, I often heard intense criticism of and 100% of the blame for the divorce placed on the ex.

No one person is completely responsible for the longevity or the failure of a marriage. A person who utters these narrow-minded statements is taking no responsibility or accountability for their divorce. They are not looking at themselves. When this person remarries, without any introspection, the second union is in jeopardy before it begins—and the ridiculous divorce stats for subsequent unions will continue to soar.

I mentioned previously one of the reasons pre-marital counseling is recommended is to examine why you were attracted to your prospective mate. The school of Analytic Psychology, founded by Freud, argues that we are attracted to certain features in a prospective mate. Some of these dynamics are known and positive but some may be unknown (unconscious) and negative. Control, for example, can be one of those unrecognized negative characteristics: The male unknowingly is attracted to a woman who seems controllable and the woman unknowingly is attracted to a powerful, controlling man. While this may seem like a match made in heaven it may not play very well in real life.

Have you ever noticed when a friend whom has recently broken a long-term relationship introduces you to their new love-interest and that person acts like and even looks much like the previous partner? People must take stock of themselves. If they don't, they will take the very same dynamics that contributed to the ruin of one relationship and put them into the next one. History will repeat itself and on and on it will go.

All these above reasons, in combination, explain why two-thirds of subsequent marriages fail. This analogy is descriptive: Some people note one of their tires on the car apparently has a slow leak. Instead of dealing with the cause of the problem they regularly put air in the tire. One day, though, they find the tire is completely flat and now they are grounded.

I strongly recommend that if you have come out of a long-term relationship, you should receive at least a year of counseling before you enter a new committed relationship. In this manner you will address any issues you may have so not to have your next relationship "go flat."

Important Points to Remember in Chapter Four

1. A major factor why subsequent marriages fail is that separated and recently divorced individuals re-couple far too quickly.
2. The same "Big 4" issues (money, sex, in-laws and kids) that plague first marriages also impact subsequent marriages—with

the added baggage of the the first union.

3. Diving into a new relationship to avoid loneliness is not the basis for a sound relationship.

4. Analytic Psychology holds that we are attracted to certain issues in our partner—which can be good or bad; this attraction can also be conscious (known) or unconscious (unrecognized). Before remarrying it is incumbent upon each partner to seek psychotherapy to prevent history from repeating and ensure they do not facilitate the collapse of another relationship.

5

How to Foster a Healthy Union

*"If you expose your genitals well before you expose your values,
the relationship is in trouble." —Waldman*

WHILE THIS BOOK is focused on divorce I would be remiss if I didn't
write at least a bit about how to develop a healthy connection and
perhaps avoid divorce altogether. My earlier book, "How Come I
Love Him but Can't Live with Him?" is primarily devoted to forming a
solid relationship and the reader is referred to it. Nevertheless, below
are tips for a successful union:

Nine Rules for a Strong Marriage

1. Select the right person.
    I know I'm repeating myself but this issue is that important.
    Remember, the right person is not the perfect person because
    no such person exists. Do yourhomework! Avoid the "deal
    breakers."

2. Go <u>slowly</u> through the courting period.
    Don't let passion cloud your judgment. Remember the
    "<u>Pyramid</u>."

3. Move from "Me to We." Forming a life-long bond with some-
    one means, I believe, you should care for that person and

their needs as much—and sometimes even more—than you care about yourself and your needs. If both parties do this, it is a beautiful thing.

For some individuals it is difficult to get past the egocentrism of our childhood and adolescence. It requires maturity to consider the needs and feelings of another person sometimes ahead of our own. By the way, this ability to place another's needs ahead of your own is what is necessary in a competent parent. (More on that later.)

4. Remember, relationships are reciprocal.
   "What you put out you will get back!" (This is psychology's version of "Garbage in; garbage out.") If you act with impatience and or anger, for example, irritability and petulance is what you likely will receive in return. On the other hand, if you demonstrate patience and understanding, your partner will most likely display the same in response. Consider this notion of reciprocity the next time you are about to be hostile, sarcastic or critical with your mate.

   When upset some folks desire to cause their partner to become as irate or more than they are. These on-going "pissing contests," pardon the expression, lay the groundwork for divorce. Appreciating how your partner may react to your message before you send it—and positively altering that message—is the hallmark of a healthy connection.

   When I worked with Nan to update her engagement ring it didn't take long before she encouraged me to update my 30-year-old BMW. (Seniors like old things.) Knowing your partner cares about your needs and wants fortifies a union.

5. Work to resolve issues.
   Don't "suffer in silence" or "store hurts." As noted previously, every relationship has a few concerns. In healthy unions the issues are managed. Instead of having an on-going war over them or suppressing your feelings only to erupt now and again when irritated, strive to communicate and settle the matter. Look for a solution that both of you are "OK" with,

that you can live with (see previous article). Knowing that you and your partner can effectively negotiate issues significantly strengthens the paring.

6. Learn acceptance.
    Acceptance is the cognitive process of recognizing an issue, realizing it is an annoyance but not a "deal breaker," understanding it is unlikely (or going to be very difficult) to change, and therefore consciously choosing to accept it. It's a step beyond tolerance. It's almost embracing the concern but choosing no longer to allow it to upset you. In this manner the previous aggravation associated with the problem is now dissipated.

    The "Serenity Prayer" applies here. It is not specifically a religious notion but a way of life. It is often said at AA meetings but it has nothing to do with alcohol—except to be able to live life without drugs:

    "God, grant me the serenity to accept the things I cannot change.

    The Courage to change the things I can.

    And the wisdom to know the difference"

7. Generate some similar interests.
    When we married Nan was much more social than me. Now, socializing with our friends is important to both of us. When we first met I was into fitness and travel more than Nan. Now, both of us enjoy working out and traveling the world.

    This is not to say that a couple has to do everything together. It is perfectly fine that a partner pursue their own hobby, for example. The couple, though, should strive to do some things together on a regular basis. Not a fan of separate vacations, though.

8. Accommodate change.
    Change will inevitably occur: job successes and failures; children and all that goes with that; family stuff; accidents; health

issues; aging, etc. Any couple married for a while will experience a host of changes which they will hopefully traverse successfully together.

Nan and I married when we were both 24. As I am writing this we are 72 and 73. Obviously we are not the same people—thank goodness. There has been lots of changes: The downs and ups of my career and Nan's as a master fourth grade teacher for 29 years; raising two sons, dealing with our sons as adults; adding two daughters-in-law and three grandkids to the family; the passing of our parents—my mother just turned 95; our aging and the aging of our friends; the passing of some good friends; our travels; etc. Being open to change is mandatory for a long-term union to survive and flourish.

9. Be willing to compromise—"Give to get."
You probably see a common thread in these tips—tolerance, flexibility, consideration etc. Being open to compromise is clearly a major example of this. In many of the couples I counselled I often saw that one partner always needed to be right and have near total control. This rarely worked. While the "weaker" partner may frequently acquiesce to the "stronger" partner there usually was resentment and passive aggressive resistance. This often led to more conflict. The ability for each partner to be willing to negotiate in good faith and compromise for the sake of the relationship will allow the union to grow. As already indicated, compromise on your part begets compromise by your partner.

I learned long ago the best way to get what you want is first to give. I live by that personally and preached it professionally. I get all I want from Nan because I give her all she wants—reciprocity and compromise.

When my sons were teens, respectively, they chided me because they saw me as a "wuss." They said, "You let Mom run everything! When I'm married I'll be the king of my castle." I responded, "We'll see what happens when you marry." Well, I bet you can guess what transpired: Each son married a wonderful, smart, strong woman—not surprisingly. They were smart. In comparison to them now, I was Tarzan!

I ran across an interesting article a few years ago in which a divorce attorney noted 12 marriage vows she wished people would make—and live by. Several of them were addressed above. Her theme was that regardless of your present mood or the current situation you should always consider the sanctity of the relationship. Don't say or do something because you're presently upset that might permanently damage the union. This is being mindful—and it's important.

Important Points to Remember in Chapter Five

Remember the nine rules for a solid union:

1. Choose the right person.
2. Slowly go through the courting period.
3. Move from "Me to We."
4. Be aware that relationships are reciprocal.
5. Strive to resolve issues.
6. Seek acceptance.
7. Develop some common interests.
8. Be prepared for change.
9. Be open to compromise—"Give to get."

6

What Divorce Looks Like to the Child

"No child ever asked his parents to divorce." — Waldman

HOW THE CHILD reacts to their parents' divorce is largely dependent on their age. An infant (0-18 months) will sense a parent is missing, especially if that parent was active in their life, and display their stress by being more fussy and eating and sleeping less. A pre-teen or adolescent obviously understands much more and may respond with anger, rebellion or possibly depression.

In a clinical case a male teen, 17, was president of his senior class, was very popular, and had one of the highest GPA's (grade point average) in his class. Brad (not his real name) was well on his way to receiving a full scholarship to a top college—until his parents announced their separation and impending divorce. He became withdrawn and depressed and began to skip classes and blow off his schoolwork. His grades began to slip.

Fortunately, his parents had the foresight to get help and sent Brad for counseling. He was very upset by the news of his parents' split and was completely blindsided by it. He poignantly stated, "If this can happen without me seeing it ahead of time, what else can happen in my life?" Like many people who experience something sudden and traumatic, Brad began to see the world differently: "Things can change without notice; the world is a dangerous, unpredictable place." He essentially developed PTSD (post-traumatic stress disorder).

Because Brad was highly intelligent, had no other major psychological issues, and was very motivated for treatment, he progressed quickly. I noted to him that what he was experiencing was perfectly normal—"a normal response to an abnormal situation." He had every right to sit in his room and grieve. However, if he chose that approach, he would likely miss out on an opportunity of a lifetime.

Brad got it and pulled himself together. He graduated second in his class and accepted a full ride to a great university—from which he graduated with honors. He sent me a few notes along his journey. The last one was to tell me he was offered another full scholarship to attend another top school to pursue a graduate degree in electrical engineering.

Clearly pre-teens, teens and even young adults will have significant emotional responses to their parents' divorce. However, children who range in age from toddlerhood, age 2-3, to ages 10-12, are probably the most psychologically vulnerable to their parents' divorce. Studies indicate that divorce, alone, does not seem to permanently harm a child's future; how the parents divorce and manage their post-divorce life seems to determine whether kids caught in divorce will have permanent problems later in life or not (Wallerstein, 1998.)

Naivete

Children are naïve. Their worlds are tiny. The infant's world consists of his/her caregiver(s), their crib and room, and perhaps a pet. The toddler's world is broader, including other care providers, grandparents perhaps, maybe a pre-school teacher, some pre-school friends, the immediate neighborhood, and a favorite park. While the toddler's world has expanded it is still quite small relative to the whole world.

Being naturally naïve and egocentric, the young child is unaware of the feelings and thoughts of others and of how others live. As far as they are concerned, their life, their reality, is the only one. Therefore, the child doesn't know if their world is good, bad or otherwise. They have no idea if they are being treated lovingly or not. The child also presumes they have the best Mother and Father possible because, again, they know nothing else. By the same token, the child can only assume that the relationship between their parents is the best ever, because this is the only union they know. Even if the parents squabble often, to the child this is completely normal.

It is not until pre-adolescence that the child begins to comprehend that there exists a much larger world than the tiny one they first knew. Moreover, it is around this time that the pre-teen or teen recognizes that their parents are not the idols they thought they were. Ironically, for the typical teen, their once perfect parents suddenly become old and out of touch and, sometimes, worse parents than all their friends possess.

How the Child Perceives Divorce

Thus, when that fateful day arrives, as the child is called into the living room, where Mom is weeping and Dad looks really sad, and Mom announces a divorce will occur and Dad is leaving tonight, never to return, the young child's world, as they know it, immediately turns upside down:

How can the perfect marriage break up?

Why is the best Father in the world being made to leave?

Aren't Mom and Dad friends anymore?

What do you mean that we have to move from the only home I've ever known?

Why do I have to change schools?

Why do I have to lose all my friends?

Did Dad divorce me, too?

Am I bad? I must have caused this?

With one parent leaving the family will I be taken care of?

I feel betrayed.

In a short time the child recognizes even more changes to his world:

Why is Mom/Dad always <u>sad</u> and cranky? Why can't I <u>fix</u> it? Am I <u>bad</u>?

Why can't I <u>see</u> Dad when I want to? Is he going to <u>abandon</u> me?

Why doesn't Mom want to <u>talk</u> about Dad anymore?

Where did all the <u>pictures</u> of Dad and the family go?

Sometimes Mom says <u>negative</u> comments about Dad? How can the <u>best</u> Mom make such statements about the <u>best</u> Dad? Who should I believe?

In some cases, even more changes occur in the child's world:

Who's this man/woman Mom/Dad is having at the house? Is he/she my <u>replacement</u> Dad/Mom?

I hate when Mom and Dad <u>fight</u>? It <u>scares</u> me. I feel <u>helpless</u>. I want to <u>fix</u> it? I must be <u>bad</u>.

Why have so many of the <u>rules</u> changed?

Like the case with Brad, just noted above, the young child is seriously <u>scared</u> and <u>confused</u> when their parents separate and divorce. Just about everything they knew to be true has <u>changed</u>. Their world has changed on a dime. They feel like they can't count or <u>depend</u> on anything. Relationships are <u>not permanent</u>. Even Dad is <u>replaceable</u>. Their world will never be the same. The world is <u>unpredictable</u>. "Without warning, apparently due to no fault of my own, the world can markedly change." With older kids there is a sense of <u>betrayal</u>— and <u>anger</u>.

I recall a clinical case involving a bight boy, 10, we'll call Todd. Todd's parents had divorced and both had remarried within a year of the dissolution (again, no great surprise). Todd experienced difficulty with all the changes. He told me this story:

He had spent the weekend with his Father and Stepmother and returned to his Mother and Stepfather on Sunday evening. Just making conversation, Mother asked Todd how the weekend went. He answered, "It was fine. We went to the zoo. Mom made spaghetti and meatballs for dinner."

With that comment Todd noted: "Jack (Stepfather) got in my face and screamed, "She's not your Mother; she's your Stepmother and don't you forget that!!" Todd started to weep.

I asked Todd, "What did you take away from that incident?" He replied, haltingly, "I – must – watch – every – word- I- say."

Out of the mouth of babes: This poor boy, in addition to all the changes that had occurred in his world within the past year, now feels he must closely monitor anything he might say in order to not offend anyone in his new family.

How much pressure can this child handle? How different is his new world? Is this fair? Imagine how he now sees his world—and his place in it. Words like <u>powerless,</u> <u>alone</u> and <u>anxious</u> immediately come to mind.

Important Points to Remember in Chapter Six

1. Parents going through divorce must be aware of how children perceive the process and do what they can to minimize the inevitable distress the child will experience.
2. Children in the midst of divorce can feel confused, scared, abandoned, helpless, anxious, hopeless, betrayed, and angry.

7 | A Healthy Divorce

"Defense attorneys see bad people at their best while divorce attorneys see good people at their worst."—Anon.

A **"HEALTHY DIVORCE"** may sound like an anachronism, like "jumbo shrimp" or "military intelligence." Nevertheless, when someone is contemplating divorce they have a choice: the easier way or the harder way. Notice, I didn't write the easy way because ending a long-term committed relationship is never easy.

What is a Divorce?

A divorce, simply stated, is the breaking of a legal contract—a marital contract. It is similar to ending a business partnership—without the kids, of course. When we marry we take vows and sign papers, which affords certain privileges—like filing taxes jointly.

The divorce process is not a war to be won. It is not to extract revenge or retribution, take all the money you can from your ex, or show the world what kind of idiot your ex was and how much of a martyr you were to have put up with them.

If children are not involved, once the division of assets (or debts) are determined both parties can essentially go their separate ways. In a few cases there may be some spousal maintenance but there will be little, if any, future contact. The relationship is over.

On the other hand, if the union produced offspring, the parties will be divorced but inextricably linked until the last child turns 18—yet will still remain connected through the children forever. Like it or not, the parties will have to "co-parent." And remember, some day there may be grandchildren.

This is where the trouble begins. If the parties couldn't make things work as a couple, how can we expect them to co-parent effectively living apart. It's amazing that the majority of divorced parents, fortunately, make it happen. Interestingly, I have noticed some parties become better parents after the divorce.

For many couples in contested divorces the legal wrangling doesn't end with the divorce. The bickering continues. Moreover, motions are filed with the Court long after the divorce was final to modify the custodial arrangement. This often requires re-hiring an attorney and returning to Court. Sadly, there are cases where motions for major changes to the custody and/or the visitation arrangements were requested more than a decade after the initial divorce was finalized.

While equitably dividing the assets and liabilities can be sticky in some cases approximately 25% of divorces including children have significant, on-going, conflict. Determining whether one parent should have full custody (total decision-making authority regarding the children) or should the custody be shared is often a major problem. (In some cases the courts may have one parent make the decisions regarding education—or perhaps religious training—while the other parent manages the medical options, for example.)

The other outstanding factor—parental access or parenting time—is often even more vexing: How much time should the kid(s) spend with each parent? Should the access be 50-50 or would the kid(s) be best served if one parent had the lion's share of the parenting time while the other parent has time, say, on alternative weekends and every Wednesday evening? In some instances the court may warrant that a parent's (briefer) parenting time be supervised—by, say, a relative or an appointed professional.

There is no doubt that in some of these cases a parent has true, legitimate concerns for their child's welfare if left alone with the other parent. On the other hand, I am completely convinced that many,

many of these contested custody cases are more about getting back at their ex than about the welfare of the child.

I recall a custody case where the Mother went on a planned 10-day vacation with her friend, leaving the 8-year-son with Father. (I warned about separate vacations). Father was always very involved in the child's care. Upon her return Mother announced she was filing for divorce. Her filing, drafted by her attorney, requested that Father have minimal parenting time and that parenting time be supervised by Father's mother.

While conducting the custody study I asked Mother to explain how was it that while married Father provided much of the child care, not to mention was the exclusive care provider during Mother's recent trip, yet upon filing for divorce Father needed to have minimal, and supervised, parenting time? Mother could not provide a convincing answer.

It was clear in this case that Mother was more interested in hurting her ex than in her child's welfare. In fact, if the Court had adopted Mother's request, the son, who had a strong, healthy relationship with Father, would have been emotionally damaged if his time with Father was severely reduced. Hence, I accused Mother of hating her ex more than loving her child (like the title of this book)—and the judge agreed.

The hallmark of a healthy divorce is, first and foremost, to keep in focus **what is in the best interests of the child(ren)**, **regardless of your feelings toward your ex**. Your ex may have been a lousy partner but that doesn't necessarily mean that they were also a poor parent. Remember, you and your ex were the only parents your kid ever knew so their concept of what constitutes excellent parenting is rather stilted anyhow.

By the same token, I had cases where a parent whom had little to do with the child while married demands joint shared custody in the divorce filing. I recall a custody case where I asked the eight-year-old boy what did he like to do with Dad for fun? Initially, he couldn't answer but after a long pause he said, "Go fishing in the park." I asked how many times he and Dad did that. "Once," was the answer. "How old were you when you did that?" I asked next. He replied, "Five, I think."

Father was resolute in having joint shared custody. I asked him several questions: "What is the name of his son's school? What grade is he in? What is his teacher's name? What is the name of his soccer coach? What is the name of his pediatrician? When is the last time you helped with his homework? Father failed the test but argued that he took his son to at least half his pediatric appointments.

As the court-appointed custody evaluator I subpoenaed the son's school and medical records—which noted which parent accompanied the child. Father had not attended one parent-teacher meeting in his son's educational career thus far and in the 18 pediatric visits I perused Father's name was not mentioned. Father's commitment to his son was minimal; he was not well-suited to effectively care for this child on a half-time basis. In some cases a parent demands joint custody primarily to not have to pay child support. This was another instance of hating the ex more than loving the kid. Children are not "trophies" to simply place on your shelf during your parenting time.

Our Adversarial Legal System

The present legal system in this country advocates that each side, each represented by an attorney, essentially verbally battles the other side in front of a judge and often a jury. (There are only judges in family law court.) Each side has their witness or expert testify to make their point and then the other side cross examines them to tear down that position. In this process the "Truth" hopefully evolves so the jury or the judge can make an informed, correct decision.

This system seems to work for criminal and civil cases (lawsuits) but it is not well-suited for divorce cases. While "the best interests of the child" are supposedly what the court is primarily seeking in contested divorce cases each parent has an attorney representing them but typically no one is representing the child. In some courts a judge will appoint an attorney to represent the child—called a Guardian ad Litem.

In criminal cases the accused is either found guilty or innocent and in a lawsuit the plaintiff (who brought the suit) is awarded damages or not. Custody cases are not so black or white. Determining the best interests of the child is not an all or nothing proposition. It's more gray. Like in the King Solomon story, you can't split the baby.

A case I had several years ago illustrates this problem: I was contacted on an emergency basis by Mother's attorney to serve as an expert witness in a divorce case that involved an 18-month old boy. Father, a physician, had left the home in Phoenix several months before and had settled into a new job with a hospital on the East coast. He already had his new girlfriend, a nurse, living with him. (Again, a common situation.)

Father's attorney petitioned the Court that Father was a good man who loved his son who could afford to give his son a good life and thus should have his son half-time (joint-shared custody—equal time and equal decision-making authority). The attorney argued that the child should spend three months at Father's residence and then switch. The judge, who was new to the Family Court, had reportedly said he would take the request under advisement but noted it "sounded fair."

I testified that the boy was bonded to Mother, a nurse on extended leave, as she was the only caretaker he knew. If he were abruptly given to Father for three months, to be cared for by Father's new love interest, the child would undoubtedly feel abandoned and traumatized. After the three months passed and perhaps the boy was just beginning to adapt to his new environment, he would be returned to Mother, only to feel abandoned again. Essentially the proposed "parenting plan" would place this child in a constant state of trauma.

What may have been "fair" to Father was absolutely unfair to this child and most certainly was not in this child's emotional best interests. Fortunately, this judge was open-minded and asked for my recommendations for an acceptable parenting plan that was appropriate for the child's developmental level. While the joint-shared custody arrangement is the default position of most family law courts today that plan may not always be the best option in all cases.

There are additional problems with the adversarial system beyond the difficulty in determining the child's best interests:

Increased Conflict, Time and Money, etc.

Theoretically, the divorce process should serve as the beginning to the end of the conflict. Unfortunately, in contested divorces, in our current legal system the conflict is escalated. All the ugliness that transpired in a failed union is paraded in front of friends, family and ex in-laws and spun by the opposing attorney. It is a most embarrassing, uncomfortable experience.

Individuals seeking retribution in divorce often find an attorney who will be more than willing to fulfill their mission to "have their day in court." Some of these attorneys make it their mission to "win," regardless if it's best for the child and despite all the conflict it brings. The angry parent is the client and is paying the fee—not the child. The traditional divorce process thus generates animosity that can linger for years—perhaps forever.

Contested divorces take a great deal of time, often with several visits to Court. Some cases continued for two years or more before they finally closed. Living in limbo for that length of time is most unsettling for parents and the children.

Contested custodial divorce cases are extremely expensive. I remember a father saying, "I could have sent both my kids to Harvard for what I spent on the divorce. Now I'm not sure I can afford a state school." Cases costing well over one hundred thousand dollars are common today. If you hire that attorney focused on fighting your fight, be prepared to finance many motion filings, witness depositions, document reviews, hired experts and additional days in Court. Often, the parent with the most funds gets their way. Family law attorneys generally make money on conflict—not peaceful resolution.

In the adversarial model the parents are largely passive. Their respective attorneys do all the talking for them, unless they are on the stand, experts give their opinions, and the judge essentially foists the final decision on the parents. I heard many times from individuals whom had recently gone through a divorce say they had little involvement in the process and absolutely no control of the outcome. I remember a frustrated father say, "It is my life but I had no say about it!"

Why Such Hate?

Attorneys commonly say there is more emotion, conflict and disgust in a contested divorce than in a civil case involving millions of dollars.

Why?

A person you once loved and procreated with may have rejected you, betrayed you and disappointed you. That creates deep hurt and resentment. But that may not be the total answer.

My theory:

Cognitive Dissonance is a term we use to describe how people think and feel. We are comfortable when our thoughts and feelings, (right or wrong), are in alignment. For example, we may have stereotypes about certain people. When we see or hear about someone who may fit our stereotype behave in a certain manner we are not surprised. To us it fits.

Suppose you are out with a long-time good friend at a bar having a few drinks and your pal begins spouting some anti-Trump rhetoric. You are a strong Trump supporter. You are now in a state of cognitive dissonance: You are most uncomfortable having a close friend who is anti-Trump.

What do you do? You could excuse your friend because she's intoxicated; change your views on Trump; or change your feelings about your friend. If you decide to change your feelings about your friend, you're all in: "She's an idiot. I don't know what I liked about her in the first place. We're done! I'm never going to see her again." You are now back in alignment.

This is what I believe operates with ex-mates. You once loved them but for various reasons you cannot love them any longer so to stay aligned you must HATE them. It is too uncomfortable to go through a contested divorce still feeling a warm spot in your heart for your ex.

Regarding that "warm spot," we have all heard of people re-marrying their ex. Thus, love can turn to hate, due to cognitive dissonance, but sometimes it can revert back to love. It has always intrigued me how close yet different the words marital and martial are.

There has to be a better way to divorce—and there is.

The Easier Way—Collaborative Divorce

It is called Collaborative Divorce or Collaborative Practice (CP). It is not mediation. It is much more. CP is relatively new. I was unaware of the concept while I was actively in practice (till 2015). CP uses a fundamentally different approach to conflict resolution. It is client-centered and focused on constructing a mutually acceptable agreement regarding assets and the children. Genuine CP staff are trained and certified by the International Academy of Collaborative Professionals (IACP). An IACP group (or two) can be found in most major cities in the US and Canada—and in other countries, as well.

How CP Works

A couple contracts with a Collaborative team. They pledge to communicate openly and civilly, in good faith, to seek a satisfactory resolution. They will not become involved with an "adversarial" attorney or with the Court during the process, as the CP contract will be terminated. Either party may cancel the contract at any time.

Each party is represented by a Collaborative attorney, who is part of the team. That lawyer is charged with addressing that client's interests and are also trained to consider the child's best interests, to facilitate communication among the participants and to help develop a reasonable settlement that the parties can live with.

An IACP team typically consists of two attorneys (at least), a mental health professional (psychologist or certified therapist), a financial professional, and often a child specialist. Often the group works out of one office but sometimes the professionals each have their own office but come together as a group for a case. Additional experts are called upon, if needed.

The mental health professional, sometimes referred to as a "coach," works to improve the communication between the parties and assist in resolving emotional issues. In some teams two coaches work individually with each parent. Each parent may choose to consult their private therapist, as long as that therapist does not interfere with the CP process.

The child specialist sees the child/ren, if they are old enough to communicate effectively. This specialist makes the parents aware of the needs and concerns of the kids and ensures the best interests of the kids are considered in the final settlement. The mental health professional and the child specialist, at times, are the same person.

The respective attorneys have several private sessions with their client, as needed. The mental health professionals, child specialist and accountant meet with both parties, as needed. Collaborative sessions include the parties and all the involved professionals. Five to eight group sessions are typically sufficient to create a mutually acceptable agreement. The settlement document is then filed with the Court and the divorce process is complete.

The agreement is designed to meet the family's needs for the long term. However, if things change, the team can meet again with the couple after the divorce.

The CP process should not be confused with mediation. In mediation the couple meets conjointly with a single mediator—usually an attorney. The mediator obviously cannot represent either party individually. Communication and problem solving techniques are typically not taught. Moreover, no one is speaking for the kids. While this process may help reduce the acrimony inherent in the traditional approach, it doesn't go as far in dealing with all the other relevant issues as in the CP process.

With the CP approach hostility is kept in check, the parties learn to communicate and problem solve effectively, the parties feel they have a voice in the process, and the best interests of the kids are preserved. A recent study conducted by the Research Institute for Law and the Family in which over a hundred Canadian family law attorneys were surveyed, found that CP takes about half the time and costs about half as much as the traditional, adversarial approach to contested divorces with custodial issues.

An IACP group can be contacted at:
info@collaborativepractice.com or 480-719-5044

Important Points to Remember in Chapter Seven

1. To divorce is to end a contract. It should not be seen as the opportunity to seek payback, retribution, or martyrdom.
2. The goal of divorce should be to divide the assets equitably and ensure the best emotional interests of the children are considered.
3. Hurt and anger can linger long after the divorce is final which will create more frustration and expense in the future.
4. The current adversarial legal approach to divorce incites anger, is lengthy, very expensive, and often fails to account for the child's best interests.
5. Cognitive Dissonance may explain why such hate occurs in divorce.
6. Collaborative Divorce may be the antidote to the ill-suited traditional approach to divorce.

Parenting through Divorce

*The best characteristic for a successful marriage is a short
memory—Anon.*

PARENTING, IN GENERAL, is one of the most difficult tasks an adult
undertakes. It is, at least, an 18-year job, but some say it never ends.
My first two books were designed to teach parents how to more ef-
fectively manage their kid's behavior: "Who's Raising Whom? A
Parents' Guide to Effective Child Discipline" and "Coping with Your
Adolescent."

Below are three published articles of mine on the subject of child
discipline:

FIVE SURE WAYS TO RAISE A RESPONSIBLE CHILD

By

Larry Waldman, Ph.D., ABPP

As an experienced clinical child psychologist, I believe the ultimate goal of any parent is to rear an independent, responsible
child. While at first glance this may appear obvious yet if we ob-
serve most parents in action on a day-to-day basis, it becomes
evident that many parents have no idea how to achieve this
objective.

Most parents never take a course on parenting or even read a book or two on the topic. Ask many parents, "How do you foster independence and responsibility in your child?" and you are likely to get a blank stare.

Our nation's future rests in the hands of our youth. It is the job of today's parents to properly raise these children. I contend that being an effective parent—and an effective spouse—are probably the two most important tasks that an adult can achieve.

Many parents believe that independence in our children occurs, more or less magically, when the child turns 18. For example, I had a case in which the father of a 17 year-ten-month-old daughter insisted that she maintain a 10:30 pm curfew. This girl, my client, was upset with her Father because this early curfew interfered with her active (and appropriate) social life. When I met with Father he argued that the curfew was in place—and would remain so—to keep his daughter "safe."

After listening to Father, I noted that his daughter, a senior in high school, would soon be attending the University of Arizona, one hundred miles away in Tucson, living in a dorm, where she would have no curfew at all. Moreover, since she would be living in a coed dorm she could have a boy in her room, if she chose. I advised Father that for his daughter to learn to become independent, like any complex skill, she needed the opportunity to practice such behavior, and he was not providing her that opportunity.

Is it any wonder why many freshmen "go crazy" when they go off to college? If the adolescent has no previous practice in behaving independently, how can we expect them to suddenly sleep right, eat right, exercise right, and make good decisions simply because they moved into a college dorm and now have no supervision?

With regard to developing responsibility, many parents mistakenly assume their task is to coerce the child to do the deed until it is complete. This process does not generate responsibility; it produces resentment and dependence in being made to do something. As I have said throughout my 40-plus year career in mental health, "If you have to make a child be responsible; they're not!"

Once I had a mother in my office yawn and apologize for being tired because she stayed up most of the previous evening completing her son's sixth grade social studies project, which he had left to the last minute. When I asked her why she did the project for him, since he chose to procrastinate, she answered, "I couldn't let him fail!"

This parent thought she was teaching her son to be responsible by getting the job done for him. Living what he learned, I assume this preadolescent is likely to continue to mismanage his time and this Mother is destined to have many more late nights "rescuing" her son.

In my many years in practice I have had dozens of cases where a freshman in college dropped out because in high school he/she was made to do their work or was rescued by their parents. In this process the teen did not learn to manage their freedom when they got to the university.

So, how do parents foster independence and responsibility in their children?

1) REINFORCE INDEPENDENT, RESPONSIBLE BEHAVIOR SPECIFICALLY AND IMMEDIATELY.

Parents tend to operate according to the "Sleeping Dog" philosophy: If the dog is quiet, leave it alone; or, if the kid is behaving appropriately leave him/her alone. What results from this skewed parenting philosophy is that the child receives essentially no parental attention for good behavior yet receives extensive parental attention for negative behavior. Then we wonder why our kids misbehave! Parents must reverse this perspective and become attuned to when their children exhibit responsible, independent behavior—and attend to it.

Most parents understand that reinforcement is intended to reward good behavior. Many parents, though, are unaware that reinforcement is also designed to educate children as to what they can

<u>do</u> when in a similar situation to earn that reinforcement again. Telling a child "good job," "way to go," or "I'm proud of you," are compliments—not reinforcement. To qualify as reinforcement the verbal praise must specifically detail exactly what the appropriate behavior <u>looked like</u>: "Billy, I like the way you brushed and flossed your teeth this morning without having me remind you. I'm proud of your independent, responsible behavior. Let's play a board game together." In this manner Billy knows exactly what he can do to get reinforced.

Reinforcement is only effective when it closely follows the targeted behavior. If an overweight person ate a reasonable meal tonight and immediately following their dinner weighed themselves and saw that they had lost two pounds, it would be easy to continue to eat in that manner. Proper eating was not that difficult because the reinforcement was immediate. Unfortunately, weight loss does not occur quickly so it is quite challenging for most people. If delayed reinforcement stymies most adults, it certainly will be problematic for children. Expecting a child to behave well on Tuesday, for example, for some reward that may occur next Saturday, is likely to be ineffective. The reinforcement must be administered immediately.

2) FOR NEARLY ONE HUNDRED YEARS RESEARCH HAS SHOWN THAT THE BEST WAY TO CHANGE AN UNDESIRABLE BEHAVIOR IS TO REINFORCE THE ALTERNATIVE DESIRED BEHAVIOR.

Often when I speak in public during the question and answer segment I am asked a question which takes the form of: "My child does so and so, which I don't like; what should I do about it?" The question portends some form of punishment.

My response to that type of question is always, "What would you prefer the child to do instead?" When I get the answer to that question, I always respond with, "Then reinforce that."

For example, if the children are squabbling in the backseat of the car while you are driving, you could scream at them to be quiet or, instead, distract them and say, "Let's play a game. The first to find five yellow VW bugs wins." In this manner, the kids learn alternative ways to behave responsibly for parental attention.

3) IGNORE MILD TO MODERATELY INAPPROPRIATE BEHAVIOR—USING "EXTINCTION"—AND ALLOW "LOGICAL/NATURAL CONSEQUENCES" TO OCCUR.

Most inappropriate behaviors that children exhibit is mildly to moderately inappropriate—like whining, procrastinating, forgetting, complaining, etc. This kind of negative behavior is done primarily for parental (negative) attention. Since most of the inappropriate behavior kids exhibit is for attention, then clearly the best response to that kind of behavior is no response. Behavioral psychologists refer to this as "extinction." When I tell parents in my office to ignore these behaviors in their children, they often look at me like I'm crazy. However, if they follow through with this concept, parents are amazed at how powerful doing nothing is.

I have recommended this "experiment" to parents for decades: "The next time your kids start to bicker, simply get up, leave the room, say nothing, go into your bedroom, leave the door open, and sit on your bed and wait." When I suggest this to parents, I often hear: "You've got to be kidding! There'll be blood on the floor! Someone will be seriously injured!"

However, what, in fact, always occurs is within 30 seconds the kids are in the parent's bedroom bringing the fight to them: "He's mean!" "She's not playing fair!" "He/she started it!" What this experiment clearly demonstrates is that, for the most part, siblings fight not because they want to maim each other but because they have learned arguing is an excellent attention-getting mechanism.

When using extinction it is imperative that parents be consistent. Don't make the mistake of ignoring the initial inappropriate behavior for a time but then later respond to it. It is predictable that when you initially ignore some behavior it will escalate briefly. Be steadfast in your extinction. If you respond to escalated behavior, you will have taught your child to become more obnoxiously persistent. If the parent is consistent, it will not take too long before the child understands the message of extinction and ceases their inappropriate behavior.

By using extinction—doing nothing—logical consequences are allowed to come into play. For example, siblings who fight and argue are left to work it out amongst themselves. The child who chooses not to complete their homework (or project) is left to be confronted by the teacher (who has received an email or a phone call from the parent saying the child behaved irresponsibly and the teacher is empowered to apply any appropriate consequence). The child who says he/she refuses to eat what is being served for dinner is simply and calmly told to leave the table. (The child is not asked, once again, "How do you know you don't like it until you've tried it," or worse yet, is made something else to eat.) The teen that gets a speeding ticket is not screamed at and grounded from driving for 60-90 days; instead, the teen is required to work off the $120.00 by doing household chores to pay for the driver re-education class he will have to attend on Saturday.

The basic components of logical consequences are that the child does not receive negative attention (and "gets their parent's goat") for misbehavior; the child learns through outside factors—not their parents' wrath—that misbehavior has its own logical/natural consequences; and, lastly, with no hysteria the child is not distracted from their misbehavior and is forced to confront their own guilt.

4) STATE THE TASK ONCE, CLEARLY AND SPECIFICALLY, AND ALLOW THE CHILD TO RESPOND. DEPENDING ON THE CHILD'S RESPONSE, FOLLOW THROUGH WITH THE APPROPRIATE CONSEQUENCE—REINFORCEMENT, EXTINCTION, OR (RARELY) PUNISHMENT.

Parents cheapen themselves. Without exaggeration I have heard at least a hundred times some parent say: "I have to tell my child at least five times before he/she will do anything." When I hear a parent say that I usually ask, "What do you think you've taught your child about your first request?"

Parent must state their request one time and allow the child to respond. Once the child has responded—good or bad—the parent applies the appropriate consequence. One of my favorite responses when one of my sons chose to ignore a task was to do that task at the same time they wanted something or needed to go somewhere. It was a great natural/logical consequence.

The parent must expect that the child will make some irresponsible choices. Which child doesn't? It's to be expected. It's part of the learning process. Consequent that poor choice and move on. Behavioral management works when the child behaves positively and is reinforced and when the child misbehaves and is appropriately consequenced.

5) IT IS NOT THE CHILD'S BEHAVIOR BUT THE PARENT'S RESPONSE TO THE BEHAVIOR THAT MATTERS.

Most parents mistakenly believe they must control their children's behavior and must make them behave. This is impossible and, moreover, puts much undo pressure on parents. Moreover, as I have said for decades: "If you have to make your kid be responsible, they're not!" An effective parent is one who systematically provides appropriate consequences to their child's behavior.

Using these five rules parents enable their children to become independent, responsible adults.

CHANGING UNDESIRABLE BEHAVIOR IN OUR KIDS

By

Larry F. Waldman, Ph.D., ABPP

Back in my undergraduate years I took a required course for all psychology majors entitled Experimental Psychology. Early in that course in a lab we were instructed to train a white rat to turn right in a T-maze. (A successful trial was defined as the rat not going past a line on the left side of the maze and the rat had to proceed all the way to the right within five seconds—to eat a small piece of compressed grain.) When the rat made five consecutive "correct" responses, it was determined that the rat had "learned" the appropriate response. I was so proud that my rodent took the fewest number of trials of the group to reach the criterion.

Once all the rats in the class had been "taught" to turn right, the issue became how many trials would it take for all the rats to "learn" to turn left (meeting the same criterion for a left turn). Three different randomly assigned conditions were used under which the rats would learn the new response: Under condition 1 the rat would receive a mild shock if they turned right (punishment). Under condition number 2 the rat would receive a mild shock for turning right but receive food for turning left (punishment and reinforcement). Under condition 3 (the one my rat happened to be in) the rat would simply receive food for turning left (reinforcement, only).

We students were asked to vote ahead of time as to what condition we thought the rats would learn the new task the fastest. The general consensus among the 40 or so undergraduate psychology students was condition 2. We were wrong. It was condition 3—by a landslide. The rats in condition 3 required statistically significantly fewer trials to all reach criterion than the rats in condition 2 and the rats in condition 2 similarly outperformed the rats in condition 1.

Upon doing the subsequent research for the write-up of this experiment it became evident that for years it had been well-documented that condition 3 (reinforcement, only) was, by far, the best way to change a behavior—with animals or children.

The research is clear: If you want to change a behavior in your child, it is far more effective to reward the alternative desired behavior than to punish the undesirable behavior. Nevertheless, despite a half-century of conclusive research, most parents punish the undesirable behavior—which the data indicates is the least effective way to change that behavior.

The next time your child misbehaves, try to ignore that behavior and attempt to arrange the environment such that the child subsequently exhibits the appropriate alternative behavior. When that occurs, be sure to reinforce it. In short time the child will be exhibiting the desired behavior consistently. (This process also works for spouses, too.)

Overindulged Children

By
Larry F. Waldman, Ph.D., ABPP

An adolescent in Texas recently was in the news for killing and/or injuring several persons due to recklessly driving his new BMW while quite intoxicated. Apparently, this teen had an alcohol-related incident a few months before this tragedy. At trial a psychologist testified that this boy should not be incarcerated because he was a victim of his parents' wealth and <u>indulgence</u>. The syndrome was coined "Affluenza." Amazingly, the judge agreed and sentenced the teen to a 120 days in a posh treatment facility.

While "Affluenza" is not a recognized diagnosis, the term does refer to a common problem today—the overindulged child:

It is often assumed that only children of rich parents are overindulged but that is not the case. Many children from families of modest incomes are also overindulged.

Parents who overindulge their kids typically are unaware they are doing anything wrong. They may be overindulgent because they were overindulged as children or they may have struggled as children and don't want their offspring to "suffer" as they did. These parents hold several false beliefs:

"I need to be my child's best friend."

"I must constantly entertain my child."

"My child requires my assistance with nearly everything."

"I show my love to my child by providing materialistic rewards."

Overindulgent parents frequently exhibit the following inappropriate behaviors:

They set few, if any, boundaries for their child.

They tolerate unacceptable behavior in their child.

They interfere with the natural consequences of their child's poor behavior.

They provide too many "toys" (like a new BMW) to their child regardless of the child's behavior.

They are overly permissive and allow too much freedom for the child at their age.

Children who have been overindulged have the following characteristics:

They test rules; rules are for others, not them.

They become dependent and non-resilient.

They lack persistence, are easily frustrated, and cannot tolerate failure.

They develop poor social skills, as they are self-centered, entitled, and demanding.

They lack empathy and appreciation.

They are easily bored.

Despite their façade of entitlement, they truly have low self-esteem.

In many respects parental overindulgence is a form of child abuse—which apparently is where the judge was coming from in the above case. Effective parents should do the following:

Set clear expectations and rules and consistently enforce them.

Insist on appreciation and consideration of the family and others.

Confront irresponsible behaviors and apply reasonable consequences.

Monitor the child's behavior and re-direct them when necessary.

Divorced Parenting

As difficult as parenting can be under "normal" conditions, parenting following separation and divorce is significantly more challenging: First, you have lost the support of the other parent (assuming you had it in the first place). Second, you are now more stressed and more burdened as a single parent. Lastly, the kids are destabilized as well.

In an earlier chapter I noted that a caring parent puts the needs of the child ahead of their own. While this concept is universally accepted, for a minority of parents going through the tumultuous process of separation and divorce their need to express their anger and frustration supersedes their commitment to their child. Their excessive emoting and venting about the other parent, to the child, can be traumatizing.

Parenting Do's (+) and Don'ts (-)

The following is a list of parenting issues specific to separation, divorce and post-divorce proceedings. The recommended approach (**Do's**) is signified by a plus (+) sign. The position some parents take, knowingly or unknowingly, which is harmful to the child (**Don'ts**) is represented by a minus (-) sign:

Prior to the Separation

WHEN TO TELL THE KIDS

+: If the child is old enough to understand, two-three days before the event inform the child that Mom and Dad made an adult decision to no longer live together and Dad/Mom will leave on, say, Friday. Answer all questions with discretion. The child now has some time to process what is about to occur.

-: Avoid ambushing the child by announcing the separation, with one parent leaving the house with suitcases, without any previous notice. The child will recall that traumatic evening as long as they live. On the other hand, don't tell the child a separation will occur "in the near future" or "next month" as the child will now obsessively brood about the event and constantly ask when and if it's happening. Remember, a child's sense of time is unlike that of an adult.

WHAT TO SAY TO THE KIDS

+: Emphasize the following to the child: A) They, in no way, caused the split. B) They did nothing wrong and are not bad. C) The departing parent is not divorcing/leaving them and they will see them often and regularly. D) They will continue to be taken care of. E) It is not their job to fix things. These points should be repeated to the child many times. This significantly lowers the stress level for the child.

-: Being so caught up in their own anguish, the parent says nothing to the child. Left with their own thoughts the child feels guilty, anxious and abandoned.

WHERE THE DEPARTING PARENT IS GOING

+: Just prior to the separation the child is taken to where the departing parent will live. The child can see the place and the room where they will sleep when they visit. The child now knows their connection to the other parent will remain intact.

-: Nothing is said regarding where the other parent is going, leaving the child to worry that their parent will be homeless or far away and they won't see them again.

During the Divorce Process

COURT/LEGAL PROCEEDINGS

+: The parent avoids speaking to the child about legal proceedings in detail as it is beyond their comprehension. Statements like "We're talking to the judge" or, if using the collaborative approach, "Mom/Dad and I are discussing things with our lawyers," are sufficient. With the collaborative process the child sees the child specialist which helps put the kid at ease. The parent assures the child their needs are being considered.

-: Telling the child about all the issues going on in Court/negotiation confuses and frightens them. Do not tell them about the final hearing day, as the child will be unable to focus on anything else the day before or the day of the trial. Finally, **DO NOT** bring the child to Court. (In a few rare cases the judge may want to interview a pre-teen or adolescent in private.)

In a case where Mother brought the child to Court, reportedly because she could not find a sitter, the judge was irate. The case did not go well for Mother, as she displayed obvious poor parental judgement.

Post-Divorce Parenting

WHERE TO RESIDE

+: Great effort is given to allowing the child to remain at their same school and stay in their same neighborhood, if the child is old enough to have friends. Also, parents strive to live close to each other, ideally within walking or easy biking distance. This allows the child to still feel some sense of order in their life.

-: Due to financial or other reasons, or failure to consider the kids' needs, the child is moved away from their school and neighborhood. This disrupts the child's education, breaks social connections and leads to additional feelings of loss and destabilization. Moreover, if the parents move far apart the visitation exchanges become more difficult and the child spends more time in the car. As the child matures and secures friendships the pre-teen/teen may become reluctant to visit their parent across town for a weekend and put themselves in social isolation for that period. This causes tension between the child and parent.

There has been a few cases where the children stay in one place and the parents move in and out. I never was involved in such a case. While this may be more convenient for the kids it is highly impractical for most parents.

The parenting plan

+: Both parents encourage frequent contact with the other parent. Each parent is open to exceptions in the schedule, if something arises. At the same time each parent strives to honor their commitment to the parenting plan, barring an emergency, which allows the child feel order in their life and lets the other parent have time to do other things. Ideally, older kids can stop in at each parent's residence at their discretion, if the parental homes are nearby. The child can relax and freely see each parent.

-: Parents adhere to a strict visitation schedule with no exceptions. Thus, if the child has a desired event, say, a birthday party, which conflicts with a scheduled visitation, the child cannot attend. If the receiving parent has a doctor's appointment, the child will have to forfeit their visit.

On a larger scale, the child is essentially banned from any extra-curricular, after-school activities (sports, theatre, dance, boy/girl scouts, martial arts etc.) because of the likely conflict with the visitation plan. The child would participate in these activities if their parents were together, yet they are excluded from them because their parents chose to divorce. The child sees their friends with intact families in these programs and feels more loss, anger and betrayal. Also, some parents are inconsistent with maintaining the schedule, which greatly irritates the other parent (which may be a part of why it happens), and causes the child to feel abandoned and unloved.

How divorced parents behave when together

+: When divorced parents are together with the child, like at an exchange, they behave in a civil, cordial manner. Mutual attendance at ball games, birthday parties, school events, etc. are common and go without incident. Again, this allows the child to relax and see the world as less dangerous.

On the other hand, there was a case where the divorced parents were so congenial with each other, it was confusing to the child. I remember seeing a girl, "Mary," 10, whom was acting out and under-achieving in school. Her parents had separated and divorced about a year before. In counseling Mary shared, "Most Friday nights Dad comes over for a big dinner that Mom cooks (like what occurred when they were together) and Mom and Dad act very nicely with each other." Moreover, Dad puts Mary to bed like he did when he lived there. I asked Mary what she thought about all this. Her response surprised me:

"If Mom and Dad can act so nice together on Friday night, why can't they still live together?" (Good question.)

In some instances people have a legal divorce but not an emotional one. I recall a case where a divorced Father remarried quickly yet called his ex nightly, reportedly to talk about the two daughters they had in common. In truth, they often discussed Mother's dates and Father's issues with his new wife (a deal breaker). It was common for Father to frequently go to Mother's house, sometimes at an odd hour, to fix something. Father's new marriage didn't last a year once his second wife recognized he hadn't emotionally detached from his first spouse.

Often the best thing to say—married or divorced—is, "I'm sorry; I was wrong; let's work this thing out." Such a statement (being honest, of course) can help greatly to overcome an impasse. The law of reciprocity applies—you get back what you give.

-: At nearly every opportunity when together with the kid the parents snipe and argue, which makes the child most uncomfortable. When in public, like at a sporting venue or even a school event, it's quite possible they will create a scene. The child is not the parents' referee. This hostility embarrasses and horrifies the child, reminding them their world has forever changed for the worse. If you walked onto an airplane and saw the pilot and co-pilot arguing ferociously, how would that make you feel?

Divorced parents never apologize and continually say and do things to upset the other parent. The fighting naturally never ends.

What divorced parents say to the child about the other parent

+: The parent strives to regularly speak positively and support-ively to the child about their other parent. They constantly remind the child that both their parents love them, care about them and want to spend time with them. This makes the child feel safe and secure.

-: The parent makes an ugly face any time the other parent is mentioned. The parent regularly speaks negatively about their ex to the child.

When a parent is disparaging the other parent to the child the kid doesn't know what to do or say. They are stuck. They are caught in what is referred to as a "loyalty squeeze." If they concur with the negative speaker, they feel disloyal to the other parent. Yet if they argue with the speaker, they are disloyal to them. Who should they believe? This position is extremely uncomfortable and anxiety-provoking for the child. Remember, before the separation the child believed both par-ents were "perfect." Ironically, the negative parent, while discharging some of their frustration, may assume they are earning some points, so to speak, with the kid. In fact, they are losing points because they are teaching the child it can be uncomfortable to be around them.

In a few cases some parents take the negativity a step further and go on a campaign to convince the child the other parent is a bad person. They speak—and spin—quite negative stories about the ex, some of which the child has no business hearing at their tender age. This is often referred to as "parental alienation." This is a sin, as far as I am concerned.

If the parental alienation is being done by the primary custodial parent, which often is the case, the child will be uncomfortable, as noted above, but essentially has nowhere to go. It is unlikely they will oppose the parent they spend most of their time with. (They aren't going to bite the only hand that feeds them.) Thus, gradually they will accept the propaganda and begin to discount and even disavow the other parent. In this condition the child will say what they believe the parent wants to hear. It breaks the other parent's heart.

I was around long enough to become involved in cases where children whom were "brainwashed" to reject a parent became an adult, and particularly after they married and had a kid, began to question why they never had a childhood connection with the other parent. When they realize that the custodial parent manipulated them and essentially stole their childhood relationship with the other parent simply to serve their anger, the young adult becomes irate. Most ironically, while the custodial parent caused the child to reject the other parent for most of that kid's childhood, once the child becomes an adult they may reject the manipulative parent for the rest of their lives, including allowing no contact with the grandkids! What a shame—everybody loses!!

I have asked manipulative divorced parents this question many times: "What do you want your kids to say about how you handled the custody issue when they become adults?" In a few cases this helped parents change their tactics. What are the odds someone raised in this deceitful manner will ultimately have a long-term healthy union? Not good.

It has been said that when a parent disparages the other parent to the child they are besmirching half of the child's genes.

Grandparents

+: By now you certainly know I strongly recommend kids have frequent access to all grandparents—your parents, your ex's parents, your new partner's parents and your ex's new partner's parents. Grandparents' love is unconditional. Once again, the more people who love your kid the better. Following the separation and divorce remind your parents that they are to speak only positively of the ex to the child.

-: Once separated some parents, typically the mother, puts a stop to the child visiting with the ex's parents, commonly the father's parents. Occasionally, those grandparents were being obtrusive by criticizing the other parent to the child. That needs to be addressed, of course. If that is not the case, the child should see their (paternal) grandparents regardless of the status of the parents' union. It is good for all: The child is loved by more people; the grandparents get to spend time with and spoil their grandchild; and the parent(s) get some time off. If grandparents use their precious time with their grandchild to badmouth the other parent, they will make the child uncomfortable (loyalty squeeze) and the child will resist going there.

I was involved in a case where the paternal grandparents had a long and lovely connection with their 8-year-old granddaughter from the very beginning. She frequently hiked with "Pops," shopped with "Nana," often ate out with them and slept over many weekends. Nana even volunteered in her class in school. When the separation was announced Mother immediately denied the child the opportunity to see Father's parents. After a few weeks Nana became depressed and couldn't stop crying. Nearly a year later the case went to Court and I testified. The Grandparents received one visit per month with one overnight. Why interrupt the healthy relationship the child had with her paternal grandparents unless you were angry and wanted to get back at Father? One more case of not loving your kid more than hating your ex.

It should be noted that once these grandkids become teens grandparents shouldn't expect that they will come around that much. How much time did you hang with your grandparents when you were an adolescent?

I would be remiss if I failed to mention that when an angry divorced parent blocks their in-laws (grandparents) from contact with the child, usually other family members, like aunts, uncles and cousins, also lose their connection to the child. Again, the total family is distressed.

Managing conflict

+: Conflict is inherent in divorce but most couples learn to "bury the hatchet" and move on. When an issue arises which one or both of the parents cannot accept, they work to create a solution. If the problem is sticky, they see a counselor. When the ex does something positive the other parent praises them. Reciprocity in relationships still operates even when the parties are divorced.

-: For some couples, sadly, the conflict is on-going. Like when they were married, any attempt to address a concern leads to an ugly exchange. Parents sometimes resort to nasty, illegal, tactics like with-holding visitation or withholding child support. This serves to fuel the anger fire. The child caught in this parental "meat grinder" continues to suffer.

Contact and visitation

+: The child is encouraged to have contact with the other parent, by phone, email, Facetime or text, within reason. The child may place pictures, notes etc. from the other parent in their room and in the house. The child thus feels connected.

Visitation with the other parent is facilitated by having clothes and toys already at the residence of the other parent so the child doesn't "have to pack" to see their other parent. For older kids having a duplicate set of textbooks and computer facilitates doing school work. It is tough enough for a child to do their school work under nor-mal conditions but it can be a tremendous additional burden to have to bring books etc. from one parental residence to/from the other.

Prior to an exchange the sending parent remains upbeat, states they are pleased the child is going to spend time with the other par-ent, and expects the child to have a good time. The child is relaxed and anticipates a positive exchange.

If possible, the exchange is made without the parents meeting. This avoids any bickering by the parents at the site. Additionally, the child doesn't have to leave the immediate custody of one parent and go directly to the other, constantly reminding them of their parents' divorce. Taking the child to school Monday morning instead of drop-ping the child at the other parent's house Sunday night or picking up the child at the after-school program instead of at the other parent's house (or some pre-arranged spot) are such examples.

-: In some homes the child is not allowed any contact whatever with the other parent. Any pictures etc. of the other parent are re-moved, as if that parent no longer exists. Of course, the child feels disconnected and alone.

The child has to "pack," like they are taking a trip, to visit the other parent. Inevitably they forget to bring something important—a piece of clothing, a favorite toy, or the book to do their homework, etc. Of course, upon their return they have left some of those items. This causes stress all around.

Some sending parents prior to an exchange present as tense and worried. They tell the child to call them immediately if anything goes wrong. They state they are going to miss them and will be lonely until they return. All of this sets a negative tone, implies to the child that the sending parent is fearful about the visit and doesn't support it, and the child is manipulated to feel guilty leaving the sending parent alone.

Parents continue to exchange the kid at the police station or post office, causing more inconvenience for all concerned.

After a visit

+: Following a visitation the receiving parent says to the child something like they hope they had a pleasant visit. This sends the child the important message that this parent wants the child to see and enjoy the other parent.

-: Sadly, when some other kids return from a visit they face an immediate interrogation focused largely on what went wrong during the visit and what mistakes the other parent is making. This procedure is most unpleasant for the child (more loyalty squeezing) and puts a damper on the visitation in general.

Years ago I worked with a gifted 10-year-old boy who said this about his visitations:

"Dr. Waldman, I was reading about World War I (he's 10!) and the Maginot Line between the French and the Germans, and it made me think. I feel like a French courier sent to the Germans to deliver a message but when I get there the Germans interrogate me fiercely. When I finally leave and return to the French they interrogate me thoroughly as well." Again, out of the mouth of babes.

With younger children it is likely they will behave a bit differ-ently for a day or so following a visitation. It is probably not because something wrong happened during the visit. It is likely the child is re-integrating, having just gone from one parent to the other and back again. It is a vivid reminder their parents are not together.

Rules

+: Ideally, the household rules before the separation should continue to apply equally in both homes after the separation. Divorced parents doing well support each other with respect to child management and discipline. For example, if the child lost a privilege at Mother's house for misbehavior, Father will sustain that consequence at his residence. By consistently maintaining the rules the child feels stabile and recognizes they can't manipulate their parents.

-: Some divorced parents change the original rules because they are too burdened to uphold them. Another reason is that a parent may feel guilty for the divorce and thus is inclined to indulge the child to (errantly) make amends. (Remember the previous article on indulged kids). Finally, some parents choose not to enforce rules to curry favor with the child and one-up the other parent. A few parents become free with money (a bribe?) or "bring home a puppy" (a classic) in the effort to induce the child to favor them over the other parent. What child will turn down money or a puppy?

Under these circumstances the child senses the world has truly changed, is likely to take advantage of the situation and manipulate the rules and strive to play one parent against the other. A favorite game older kids like to play is if one parent applies some discipline, the child complains to the other parent, hoping that parent will rescind the punishment. Don't fall for that! Instead, increase the penalty to put an end to that ploy. If parents don't manage the child well after divorce, they will have an upset <u>and</u> a poorly behaved kid.

Child as confidante

+: As already fully discussed, separation and divorce puts the entire family at risk emotionally. Nevertheless, the competent parent does not change the basic nature of the parent-child relationship.

-: Hurting emotionally and without a partner to commiserate with, some parents use their (older) child as a confidante. They discuss personal, adult issues and intimate details of the divorce with the child. The child will gladly receive the attention but the information is inappropriate and the relationship is altered, as the child now feels more like a peer than a kid. When the parent subsequently asks the child to clean their room the child may balk because peers don't do chores. Once again, the child recognizes how much their world has changed. Also, some of the shared adult information may well be upsetting to the child and/or beyond their comprehension to process it appropriately.

Child as spy

+: It is natural to wonder how your ex is doing. However, the mature parent doesn't involve the child in that question.

-: Some divorced parents hope their ex is struggling (like they may be), want to know if their ex is seeing someone, and how they are doing financially. To answer those questions the parent enlists the child to do reconnaissance during their visit with the other parent and report back to the parent. This puts the kid in a bind (again, the loyalty squeeze) because to which parent are they to be loyal? Moreover, the other parent, aware of this "game," may warn the child they are not to say anything substantive about the visit to the other parent. Now the poor kid is really in a pickle.

Imagine the stress this poor child has to endure. When this kid becomes a teen there will be hell to pay!

Child as messenger

+: A mature divorced parent communicates directly and cordially with their ex and does not involve the child.

-: Some divorced parents, out of fear of another ugly conversation, or, perhaps, to embarrass the ex, use the kid to convey a message—especially a negative one. "The child support check is late. We need to buy some food," for instance. Once more, the child is caught between his parents—the kid can't win. Also, the parent receiving the message is irked.

I recall a pre-teen relate this story in a therapy session: "Dad often brought me home late on Sunday (night, after a visit). Mom complained to the Court and the Judge said Dad had to get me home on time. So we're out (on a Sunday) having fun but Dad realizes we're going to be late again (getting back to Mother's house on time).

So Dad calls Mom, gives me the phone, and tells me to tell Mom we're going to be late. I didn't know what to do. Mom was going to be mad. Mom answers and I tell her we're having fun but we're late. She screams at me, calls Dad a bunch of names and hangs up. Dad then asks what she said. And I started to cry."

The unrelenting pressure and angst that some divorced parents place upon their children causes indelible consequences.

Dating after divorce

+: Divorced parents need to have a social life. They should occasionally go out with friends to relax, be with adults and get a break from single parenting. Casual dating is ok.

As discussed, the recently-divorced parent should be in counseling. The counseling goals are to re-integrate, understand their role in the divorce, learn what to look for and look out for in another partner, how to communicate with their ex, and learn to effectively deal with the kid(s).

While casually dating you should meet that person away from your home so the child doesn't ponder if that person will become their stepparent. Remember, that first year following divorce is not the time to get into a committed relationship.

After a year or so, once you have settled in and completed your counseling, if an exclusive relationship is developing, the parent must fully vet their new love interest and also assess their capability to properly parent your kid(s). Then, and only then, should your prospective partner be introduced to your kids.

Next there must be numerous opportunities for your "friend" to interact with your child to determine if they are a suitable stepparent and a decent fit with your child. You are essentially seeking a match with your new partner and a match between your partner and your child—twice the work. If your friend also has a kid, you must additionally assess the match of that child with yours.

There was a case where a divorced mom met and vetted, she thought, a divorced dad and formed a nice relationship. Each had a young son. She had full custody of her son and he had shared custody of his boy. When they finally moved in together to form a new family she quickly realized that his son was seriously emotionally disturbed and bullied and terrorized her son. His ex, whom had medical decision authority, refused to seek help for the kid. This divorced mom had no choice but to end the relationship. The vetting must be thorough.

Once the family is living comfortably under one roof the children must be instructed that each adult now has equal parenting/discipline authority. Family counseling would be useful here.

Hopefully, your ex will recognize you carefully and wisely selected a new partner and step-parent for the kids and is supportive. At the same time, if your ex has recoupled, unless that person is abusive to your kids, you speak favorably of that individual to the children, as well.

When the new partner becomes part of the family the parent does not expect the child to immediately love that person or call him/her Mom/Dad. Over time the child may, or may not, do that on their own.

-: Needing to relax and desperately seeking attention and confirmation, the newly divorced parent goes out frequently, often leaving the child with a sitter. The child feels alone. The parent is disinterested or too busy to seek counseling.

The parent introduces each date to the kid. The child wonders every time: Is he/she going to be my replacement parent? The child is confused.

The parent rushes into the next relationship. Essentially no vetting is done. The new partner moves in, having had little or no previous contact with the child. The child is uncomfortable with this stranger living with them and sleeping with their parent. They are also upset that this person is replacing their other parent and is resentful of the time and attention this person is receiving from their parent at their expense. The relationship between the child and their parent's new friend is clearly off to a rocky start.

The child quickly finds this new person is rather "bossy" or, conversely, this person seems to have little interest in them. Whenever the child asks a question or makes a request this person's reply always is, "Ask your parent." The child recognizes this person has no discipline interest or authority.

If kids come with the new person, each adult is responsible only to their child, which creates jealousy and much disorganization in the home.

The child complains about this person to their other parent during a visitation. That parent now confronts the ex about what is going on, adding to the conflict between them. The parent now confronts the child for speaking to the other parent, telling them to keep quiet. The child is unhappy and feels trapped.

The odds of this family constellation remaining intact are low—and the kid may have to go through this process once again, perhaps with the other parent and their new partner, as well. It becomes easy to understand why kids caught in this mess begin to see their worlds as crazy and unsettled.

Perhaps angry, and maybe a bit jealous, when you learn that your ex has found another partner, you criticize that person to the children. Sometimes you suggest that person was the cause of the divorce in the first place—which may or may not be true. The kids are encouraged to share anything wrong that person does. Worse yet, the kids are reminded that this person has no real parental authority so they don't have to listen to them.

This tactic causes tension at the other home and infuriates the ex, causing them to seek payback—reciprocity. Additionally, in many cases the kids are once again caught in that "loyalty squeeze" because if they show disdain to the new partner, they are loyal to one parent but not the other; conversely, if they like the new partner (and often that is the case) they are now being disloyal to the other parent.

This all too common dirty trick causes much angst in divorced families and considerable distress to the children. When the kids become adults they will look very unfavorably toward the parent that put them in such an untenable position.

Services for the child

+: Mature divorced parents with joint-shared custody cooperate and collaborate with the child's doctor, dentist, teacher and coach.

-: Every medical, dental, educational, athletic decision etc. presents the opportunity for the parties to squabble. This interferes with the child's education and health care and is most embarrassing to the kid. If divorced parents are unable to agree on these issues, shared custody may not be appropriate for that family. Often the real issue is that each parent refuses to do what the other parent suggests. Obviously, this is unfair to the child.

Important Points to Remember in Chapter Eight

1. Divorced parents should read information on general parenting.
2. The child should not be ambushed on the night of the separation.
3. The child should see where the departing parent will reside.
4. The child should not be burdened with the legal proceedings.
5. The child is best served if both parents live close by and can attend the same school with the same friends. Seek counseling.
6. Parents, and their family members, are to speak supportively of the other parent.
7. The parenting plan must be flexible.
8. A set of the child's clothes, toys and school books should exist at both houses.
9. The child is not a referee, confidante, spy or messenger. Seek counseling.
10. A parent's new friend should be introduced to the child once the relationship is exclusive.
11. If the friend moves in, perhaps with kids, both parents have equal discipline authority of all kids. Seek counseling.
12. Show support to the kids of the ex's new partner.

9

Finding the Right Counselor

"A happy marriage is the union of two good forgivers."—RB
Graham

THROUGHOUT THIS BOOK I have recommended counseling. An experienced, well-trained family therapist, familiar with divorce and the related legal issues ("forensically sensitive") can help immensely. A good therapist should support you but also challenge you by questioning some of your "stinkin thinkin," as I like to call it. A clinician may also point out some of your maladaptive behaviors and assist you in modifying them. A competent couples counselor will stay neutral and strive to help the parties resolve troublesome issues. Frankly, I contend everyone could benefit from seeing a psychotherapist at any difficult time in their life—or more.

The Stigma of Mental Health

There still remains a stigma in our society today associated with seeking psychological help, although it is getting somewhat better. I find this view to be short-sighted since the data clearly shows that better than 20% of the US population will deal with depression or anxiety in their lifetime.

Why is it OK to see a specialist, say, for your heart, back, or stomach, yet it is somehow shameful to consult someone about your mind? This puzzles me. (Maybe I should see a counselor.) The mind and body are connected. It is ludicrous to treat one but not the other. You are not considered weak or bad if you get help for your aching back. Why, then, should you feel shame or embarrassment to receive psychological assistance.

Some people believe you have to be "crazy" to see a mental health professional. In truth, crazy—psychotic—individuals rarely seek their own treatment. As noted earlier, going through a separation and divorce is one of the most stressful things a human can do. Going through that experience without the assistance of a mental health provider, in my view, is crazy.

This stigma keeps many people from the mental health treatment they need. I can't tell how many times I heard someone say, "I don't need counseling; I'm not crazy." My response is: You're right, you aren't crazy but you are in need of counseling." At least 30 times in my career a wife came in for marital therapy without her husband because he refused to participate in the counseling—due to shame or it's all the wife's fault, etc. He would spend a great deal of time and money to fix the transmission in his truck but won't spend a minute or a dime to save his marriage. Interestingly, after I worked with the wife and things got somewhat better at home many of those reluctant husbands, noticing the positive change, decided to come in. It is time that mental health treatment be fully and openly accepted.

The following true story illustrates my point: More than a decade ago I was called as a witness in a custody modification case. Mother had full custody of the child and Father wanted the custody changed. Father learned that Mother had recently seen me for child management counseling and subpoenaed me to appear in court.

Father's attorney argued that since Mother had to seek psychological services to better manage the child's behavior she obviously was an unfit parent. Custody of the child, therefore, should be awarded to Father.

On the witness stand I said I could not compare Mother's suitability as a parent with that of Father's because I had never met him. However, the position that Mother was automatically unfit because she sought parenting guidance was, in my view, stupid: If the child had a broken limb and Mother had refused to take him to a specialist, the case would be made that Mom was remiss in her duties as a parent. On the other hand, if Mother seeks the services of a specialist for a behavioral issue with her son, she is deemed unfit. The fact that Mother recognized that she had a problem and decided to get help was, in my view, a sign of love and caring and an indication of good parenting.

Father, and his attorney, hoped the judge would see Mother as incompetent and bad because she had to consult a psychologist regarding the child. Nevertheless, the case was dropped and the mother retained custody of the child. The judge viewed Mother seeking parenting guidance for a child caught between conflicted divorced parents as quite appropriate.

Mental Health Treatment in a Pill

I view today's health care system as focused essentially from "the neck down." Not enough attention is given to the mind. If someone does access the health system for a mental health concern, the odds are high they will get a pill only. Below is an article of mine on that subject:

There is No Education in a Pill

By

Larry F. Waldman, Ph.D., ABPP

Psychologist

The reasons for the current opioid epidemic are due to the following, largely unspoken, reasons:

Physicians don't have the time (and training) to effectively deal with their patients' pain.

Insurance companies prefer the quick, simpler treatment through medication over other longer, more complex non-medical interventions.

Our nation's health insurance and drug companies have

masterfully convinced most consumers and many providers that the majority of health care issues can be resolved with a pill, tablet or capsule.

When in pain you want fast relief. Caring physicians want to provide it. In many acute situations, like an accident or coming out of surgery, a <u>brief</u> regime of powerful pain medication is appropriate. On the other hand, when the pain is long-standing—such as a "bad back"—the long-term use of strong, addictive pain medications (analgesics) is decidedly dangerous.

Oxycodone, a common analgesic, is chemically quite similar to heroin—and today heroin on the street is much cheaper. Oxycodone is an addictive drug. Initially it masks the pain well. The patient is highly reinforced by the drug, medically and psychologically, as it eases the pain, may provide a sense of euphoria and may even promote sleep—at least early on.

Like any addictive drug it creates a "tolerance"—where more of the chemical is needed to get the same initial effect. Thus, patients on such pain meds over time require more and more of the drug. Many times people continue to take the medication, even after the original injury has healed, because they want to ensure they have no pain, they like/need the psychological effect of the drug, and they may go through withdrawal (which can be quite unpleasant) if they abruptly stop the drug. The real danger is that not only will high doses of "Oxy" stop pain, it will stop your heart.

As the patient begins to significantly overuse their pain meds, sooner or later their MD will stop prescribing it. This will create a crisis: I have seen good people forge prescriptions, borrow meds from family and friends, go into medicine cabinets of others and steal meds, buy "Oxy" on the street and even purchase heroin. Now you're facing death and/or the possibility of ruining your life.

This opioid issue is the tip of the iceberg of a bigger issue, I believe. The US health care system, while the most expensive, ranks below Australia, Canada and most other European nations. Moreover, for the first time in history it was just announced that the average life expectancy for a US citizen went down (one-tenth of a year). Clearly, what we are presently doing isn't working.

As a long-term health care provider, I remember when insurance companies simply paid for care—and they still made nice profits. Today they direct the care. It's a classic case of the tail wagging the dog. (This is why your family doctor today can only afford to give you seven minutes of their time.) Our nation's health must be guided by health professionals not by CPA's, MBA's and CFO's.

Acupuncture, acupressure, biofeedback, occupational therapy, physical therapy, Pilates, meditation training, therapeutic weight loss, therapeutic massage, yoga, and, of course, psychotherapy, are all forms of non-medical treatments for pain. While they may be more expensive initially they are not addictive or dangerous. Moreover, these treatments educate the patient how to manage their pain beyond taking a dangerous drug.

Similarly, learning to manage depression and anxiety—the two most common mental health issues—with psychotherapy to change thoughts and behaviors is essential for long-term results. Meditation, exercise, yoga, and weight loss can also useful. Nevertheless, the usual treatment today for depression and/or anxiety is a prescription for an anti-depressant and/or a tranquilizer—which also is habit- forming. Medication certainly is useful in some situations but it absolutely should not be the sole response to these concerns.

The next time your physician recommends medicine for your pain, depression or anxiety ask—no demand—that your MD also write a prescription for some other appropriate non-medical intervention as an adjunct treatment. Remember, there is no education in a pill.

PhD/PsyD, MFT, MA, LPC, MSW, MC, NP or MD

With all these initials floating around the mental health field ("alphabet soup") it is rather confusing to the average consumer. Some people don't understand the difference between a psychologist and a psychiatrist and even fewer people can differentiate between a psychologist (PhD/PsyD), marriage and family therapist (MFT), counselor (MA, LPC or MC), clinical social worker (MSW) or psychiatrist (MD).

Psychiatrists are medical doctors, attended medical school, and have completed a psychiatric internship in mental health, specializing in children or adults. They prescribe psychotropic medication. Psychiatric NP's, nurse practitioners, attended nursing school and also prescribe such medication.

Psychologists have a master's and a doctoral degree (Ph.D. or Psy.D.) from a graduate school of psychology. To add to the confusion, some psychologists have additional training in psychopharmacology and can also prescribe medication in several states—currently New Mexico, Illinois, Iowa, Idaho and Louisiana (and in the military).

MFTs, MAs, LPCs, MCs and MSWs typically have a master's degree from a graduate school of counseling, psychology, education or social work. Some colleges offer doctoral degrees in social work—DSW's.

Obviously I'm in favor of using psychologists but, in truth, what truly matters in psychotherapy is the clinician's training, experience and professional rapport that provider develops with the clients. (Psychiatrists, nurse practitioners and some psychologists refer to their customers/clients as patients.) Generally speaking, the training most psychiatrists and nurse practitioners (NPs) receive today is focused more on pharmacology than psychotherapy. Thus, unless you are considering medication, I don't recommend a psychiatrist or NP as a marriage counselor.

Where to Find your Counselor

First, ask your family physician, pediatrician or OBG for a referral. Most likely they have had many previous patients who requested a marital therapist so they should be familiar with the work of one or more counselors. You might also ask a friend if they had or know of a good marital therapist.

Your insurance carrier probably has a list of providers in their network. All of the previously mentioned professionals belong to their state and local organizations. Many of these associations have an I & R (Information and Referral) service. Finally, there is always the internet.

What to Look For

I recommend you find a provider that has been in practice at least five years, is specifically trained in marital therapy, and has worked with at least 50 couples. I prefer a behavioral, solution-focused approach. If they are certified by Dr. John Gottman, or at least is familiar with his work, that would be especially nice. I always saw the couple together when I did marital therapy.

Ask These Questions

When you have a referral contact the office and ask to speak briefly (no more than 5 minutes) with the therapist to ask the following questions. This is not the time or place to discuss your case. You might find the answers to these questions below on the therapist's web site.

1. How long have you been in practice?
2. Are you specifically trained in marital therapy?
3. How many couples have you worked with?
4. What is your approach and theoretical orientation?
5. Are you familiar with Gottman's work?
6. Do you take my insurance?
7. Do you have family court experience?

If you cannot reach the therapist, and the website is not useful, speak with the office manager. If they can't answer all your questions, ask them to speak with the clinician and get back to you. (This would be good information for the office manager to know, anyhow.)

Below is an article I wrote on this subject:

Shopping for Mental Health Care

By

Larry F. Waldman, Ph.D., ABPP

When we enter a grocery store or our primary care physician's office we generally know what kind of service we will receive. For most of us this is not the case when we begin treatment with a mental health provider. During my career I met many frustrated clients who complained that their previous mental health practitioner failed to offer medication, recommended medication, talked too much, or too little. Unfortunately, we are poor consumers with respect to mental health care. We spend more energy researching a purchase for a household product than selecting our mental health provider.

In truth, the mental health field is certainly confusing and, should I say it—crazy. Providers primarily are psychiatrists, psychologists, nurse practitioners, marriage and family therapists, counselors, social workers, and, more recently, life coaches. Basic forms of treatment include psychopharmacology (medication), psychoanalysis, family of origin work, family therapy, behavior therapy, EMDR, and coaching. Obviously, it is quite confusing for the typical consumer to differentiate among the various providers and therapies.

To make matters worse, there are four basic approaches or perspectives regarding the definition and treatment of mental health issues—the biological, analytic, cognitive, and behavioral schools. Each school has its own view on how psychological issues develop, how they are sustained, and how they should be treated.

Mental health practitioners typically follow the perspective that was prominent in their graduate training. They tend to become more eclectic in their approach with time and experience. I submit most providers offer the form of therapy that best suits their own personality. Consumers usually have little knowledge regarding these four perspectives and very few providers advertise their professional orientation.

If someone was seeking services for anxiety, a common referral issue, for example, and saw a professional who subscribes to the Biological school (a psychiatrist or nurse practitioner) the patient likely would receive a prescription for medication. If they saw a provider who adheres to the Analytic view (typically a psychiatrist or psychologist), they would spend much time discussing their childhood.

If the client connects with a Cognitive therapist (psychologist, therapist, counselor, social worker) they would be helped to identify and change their negative, self-defeating thoughts. Finally, if the individual sees a provider who identifies with the Behavioral perspective (psychologist, counselor, therapist, coach), they will be taught to face their fears.

Research has not found that one approach is consistently better than another. What seems to be critical is the proper connection between the client/patient and the provider. I recommend the following:

Do some research on the four schools of thought and try to determine which approach is most appealing to you.

Check out your prospective provider on the Internet to see if their professional orientation is described. If it is not available, call the office manager and request it. Don't be surprised if the manager is unaware of the provider's perspective but then ask the manager to get it and get back to you. (This could educate the office help, too.)

Make an appointment with a provider that you believe will be a good fit. Just because a clinician is located around the corner or takes your insurance does not mean they will be best for you.

If the treatment does not seem to be helping, speak about it with your provider; that discussion could be quite therapeutic. Don't just stop coming if you are dissatisfied with the process. If no progress is made after that discussion, find another professional. (We usually try a few mechanics or hairstylists before we find one we like; the same may be true with mental health providers.)

Be a Good Client/Patient

Keep your appointments. Come on time. Do your assigned homework. Pay your bill. Communicate with your therapist. If progress is too slow, discuss it in the next session. After noting your concerns with the therapist and little has changed, find a new counselor.

My hope is that if you have read to this point, you will accommodate your ex as much as you love your child. Put aside your anger and communicate with your ex, for the sake of your child. They will forever love you for that.

Good luck.

Important Points to Remember in Chapter Nine

1. Don't let the narrow-minded stigma regarding mental health treatment prevent you from seeking personal or marital counseling.
2. Marital counseling rarely involves psychotropic medication unless one one of the parties is seriously depressed or anxious.
3. Don't get lost in the "alphabet soup" of mental health providers.
4. Locate a counselor for yourself or as a couple from your family
5. physician, pediatrician, OBG, friend, insurance panel, association I & R, or Google.
6. Ask questions of the therapist before scheduling an appointment.
7. Be a good client/patient.

Bibliography

Agape-aid.org/relationship stages-infatuation. <u>Saving a Marriage.</u> 2019 Anderson. J., The Impact of Family Structure on the Health of Children: Effects of The Linacre Quarterly, November, 2014.

CDC, Centers for Disease Control and Prevention

Darnell, D. <u>Beyond Divorce Casualties: Reunifying the Alienated Family</u>, Taylor rade, Lanham, MD, 2010.

Gottman, J. <u>The Seven Principles for Making Marriage Work</u>, Harmony Books, New York, 2015.

Leininger, C. The 12 <u>Wedding Vows Your Divorce Attorney Would Write for You</u>, candiseleininger@aol.com, November 12, 2014

Mastracci, M. <u>Divorce without Dishonor: Stop Fighting Over the Kids</u>, St. Gabriel's Press, Baltimore, 2009.

Nocera, T. ParentalWisdom.com

Paetsch, P., Bertrand, L., & Boyd, J., <u>An Evaluation of the Cost of Family Law Disputes</u>, Canadian Research Institute for Law and the Family, December, 2017.

Robin, E. AFriendlyDivorce.com

Sedacca, R. ParentingBeyondDivorce.com

Waldman, L. <u>Who's Raising Whom? A Parents' Guide to Effective Child Discipline</u>, UCS Press, Phoenix, 4th Edition, 2007.

Waldman, L., Coping with your Adolescent, Hampton Roads Publishing Co., Norfolk, VA, 1994.

Waldman, L. How Come I Love Him but Can't Live with Him? How to Make Your Marriage Work Better, Minuteman Press, Milwaukee, WI, 2002

Wallerstein, J., The Long-Term Impact of Divorce on Children, Courts Law and Families, 1998.

Weiner-Davis, M. Healing from Infidelity, Michele Weiner-Davis Training Corp., Woodstock, IL, 2017

Other Books by Dr. Waldman

Who's Raising Whom? A Parent's Guide to Effective Child Discipline.

Coping with Your Adolescent

How Come I Love Him but Can't Live with Him? How to Make Your Marriage Work Better

The Graduate Course You Never Had: How to Develop, Manage and Market a Flourishing Mental Health Practice—With or without Managed Care

Too Busy Earning a Living to Make Your Fortune? Discover the Psychology of Achieving your Life Goals

Overcoming your Negotiaphobia: Negotiating your Way through Life.

Dr. Waldman Speaks

To the Community and Corporations:

Who's Raising Whom?

Parenting through Divorce

Effective Stress Management

Managing Depression and Anxiety

7 Reasons Why We Fail to Achieve our Life Goals and How to Overcome Them

To Mental Health Professionals:

The Business of Private Practice: The Graduate Course You Never Had

Counseling Parents to Raise Responsible, Resilient Kids

Producing, Publishing and Promoting your Book

To Attorneys:

Recognizing and Managing PTSD in the PI Client

Parenting through Divorce

About Dr. Waldman

Larry F. Waldman, Ph.D., ABPP
Psychologist, Speaker

Dr. Waldman is a recently semi-retired certified school psychologist and licensed clinical, forensic psychologist in Phoenix, Arizona. He conducted a highly successful private practice of 45 years working with children, teens, parents, couples, and adults in a solution-focused manner. He also consulted with family, personal injury, immigration and estate planning attorneys. His BS in Education/Psychology was from the University of Wisconsin; his MS in School Psychology was from the University of Wisconsin-Milwaukee; his Ph.D. in Educational/School Psychology was earned at Arizona State University; and his Diplomate (ABPP) was received in 2003.

Waldman was the past president of the Maricopa Psychological Society, the Director of Psychological Services for Charter Psychiatric Hospital of Glendale and was an "Official Guide" (top expert) on Parenting for SelfGrowth.com. He continues as a Medical Consultant for the Social Security Office in Phoenix, an adjunct graduate professor in the Counseling and Educational Psychology Departments for Ottawa University, and serves on the professional advisory board of Stepping Stones of Hope, a charitable organization serving children whom have lost a parent. Waldman is the co-chair of the Early Career

Psychologists Committee with the Arizona Psychological Association (AzPA). He is also certified by the American Council on Exercise (ACE) as a (senior) fitness specialist.

In addition to numerous articles which have been published in the local Phoenix media and in the national press, Waldman has (thus far) written six books: *Who's Raising Whom? Coping with Your Adolescent; How Come I Love Him But Can't Live with Him? The Graduate Course You Never Had; Too Busy Earning a Living to Make Your Fortune?* and *Overcoming Your Negotiaphobia: Negotiating Through Your Life.* He currently is writing *Love your Kid More than You Hate your Ex.*

Dr. Waldman trained as a public speaker. His signature presentations are: **The Business of Private Practice—The Graduate Course You Never Had** and **Teaching Parents to Parent.** He has made over 150 paid presentations in his career to attorneys, chiropractors, psychologists, family therapists, counselors, social workers, school psychologists and school counselors. To the community Waldman speaks on parenting, marriage, stress, depression and anxiety, wellness, grandparenting and psychotherapy. His seminars are organized, practical and entertaining—offering "**edutainment**."

Contact Dr. Waldman

larrywaldmanphd@cox.net

602-418-8161

5061 E. Cortez, Scottsdale, AZ 85254-4634

TopPhoenixPsychologist.com

Lightning Source UK Ltd.
Milton Keynes UK
UKHW021800260421
382664UK00007B/1011